POWER SPOTS

A unique and challenging introduction to our relationship with the Earth itself, which reveals how we can 'ground' ourselves as natural beings and, by working with natural forces, develop a deeper knowledge of ourselves and our environment.

Also by Nathaniel Altman
THE PALMISTRY WORKBOOK
SEXUAL PALMISTRY

POWER SPOTS

A unique guide to contacting inner and outer
energy points that will transform your life

JOSÉ ALBERTO ROSA MD

with

NATHANIEL ALTMAN

*Photographs by
Eleni Mylonas*

THE AQUARIAN PRESS
Wellingborough, Northamptonshire

First published 1986

British Library Cataloguing in Publication Data

Rosa, José Alberto
    Power spots: a unique guide to contacting
    inner and outer energy points that will
    transform your life.
    1. Psychotherapy   2. Psychical research
    I. Title   II. Altman, Nathaniel
    616.89'14   RC480.5

ISBN 0-85030-474-1

*The Aquarian Press is part of the
Thorsons Publishing Group*

Printed and Bound in Great Britain by
Whitstable Litho Ltd., Whitstable, Kent

This book is dedicated with gratitude to my three teachers,
Alexander Lowen, M.D.
Theda Basso
Paulo de Campos Mattos (Paulinho)

CONTENTS

ACKNOWLEDGEMENTS

The authors would like to thank the following people whose inspiration, editorial assistance, suggestions and support were crucial to the successful completion of the manuscript: Robert K. Altman, Sadie Davis Altman, Marjorie Bair, Paulo Bopp, Linda James, Clara Lorenzi, Maria Teresa Santos.
We are also grateful to Shelli Goldstein and Matthew Steuer for serving as models for the exercises presented in Chapter 4.

INTRODUCTION

We left my office in four cars. Our destination was a small country hotel in the region of Visconde de Mauá, some four hours south-west of Rio de Janeiro. As a psychiatrist who integrated traditional psychotherapy with bodywork (opening of energy blocks through the release of chronic tensions in the body with special physical exercises and deep tissue massage) this was my first workshop outside the rigid confines of an office or school. For this reason, the prospect of a weekend in nature was very exciting to me, and our destination, suggested by a colleague, was said to have a dynamic energy all its own.

The journey along the modern expressway towards São Paulo was fast and relaxing, but the unpaved road from the superhighway to Visconde de Mauá was filled with potholes and washouts, making travel quite difficult. By nightfall we had arrived at the hotel, a cozy wooden structure perched high in the mountains next to a rushing stream and waterfall. My colleague was right — the energy there was serene and yet highly charged. I knew that we had chosen the right place for our workshop.

After a sauna, a cold shower under the falls and dinner at the hotel, the ten of us started to work, focusing on physical exercises to open up a better flow of energy in the body. As a group leader, I had often experienced that individuals working in a group create a cohesive and collective energy. This evening, after an hour of dynamic movement and exercise outside the hotel, I felt that the group's energy had reached a 'primal' cohesiveness with a life force all its own.

We soon moved on to an exercise designed to help each individual reach a deeper psychological level. The exercise featured a technique that would help the participants become aware of how and what they were feeling at that very moment. By opening the door to these often hidden emotions and feelings, we would be able to set the direction for each individual's work during the rest of the workshop.

The technique I used involved spinning each person around rapidly, with eyes closed. We gradually slowed the spinning down until the person sensed a particular direction to follow. I suggested that each person walk, with eyes half closed, in the direction of his choice, and call out his name over and over. This was to continue until the individual felt that he had arrived at the spot to which he was instinctively drawn. Upon arriving at the spot, he was instructed to relax, become familiar with the terrain, and otherwise 'get in touch' with his spot, so that he would open himself to whatever impressions might be found there.

The exercise took approximately three hours. When I walked around to check on each participant, I found that one woman was embracing a tree, quietly sobbing. I found two of the men sitting on large rocks in a state of deep meditation. I then came upon a woman standing knee-deep in the stream, with open arms, her body swaying back and forth in a trancelike rhythmic state. One of the participants managed to completely hide himself in a small cave by the stream, where I found him chanting and singing loudly. As I continued my walk, I found that others were experiencing their own special contact with nature. Although at the time I felt that their reactions were largely psychological, it was obvious that this exercise had had a profound effect on everyone.

Later on, we shared our experiences together as a group. Although the psychotherapist in me was busy analysing their experience, I could hear a voice within me saying 'These are their power spots and also the home of each person's *orisha*.'

I had read about power spots in the first two Carlos Castaneda books* and understood them to be places in nature which contain a high concentration of benign, protective energy. They are said to be highly conducive to meditation and inner healing. However, I knew very little about orishas (pronounced oar-ee-shahs') which is a type of being known as a nature spirit or *deva*. At that time I only knew that orishas played a role in a Brazilian religion called *Candomblé* that works with the powers of nature. Even though I was sceptical about Candomblé as a religion, it was clear that by making contact with the orishas and power spots, I had touched on something very important which I would have to pursue further.

We spent the following day inside the hotel, working both psychologically and energetically as a group. The next morning I felt that we should again go back to nature, so I took the group to a secluded area deep in the woods. In addition to several groups of tall, majestic trees, our surroundings included high cliffs, a rushing stream with waterfalls, a broad meadow filled with wild flowers, and numerous large outcroppings of rock.

I split the group into two so that each member would have the assistance of a helper or guide. The first group of four then started the process of finding their power spots, using the technique employed two days before. They would be followed by their partners to their power spots; the partner would later come back to tell me where they were. After returning to the power spot of their friend, they would

---

The Teachings of Don Juan: A Yaqui Way of Knowledge and *A Separate Reality: Further Conversations With Don Juan* (New York: Simon & Schuster).

assist in helping the person do deep breathing and meditation until I would come to work with them.

I then visited each person at his power spot, and began working with them both psychologically and energetically. Like the first evening, the process each individual went through was very deep and often quite dramatic. During their sessions in their power spots, several came upon important discoveries regarding their psychological or spiritual nature, while others received a clear vision to help them resolve a specific issue concerning work, study or relationship. By the end of the workshop, I realized that both the energetic and psychological work had had much more power and focus than similar work done in the office. I perceived in my clients a greater degree of courage, a deeper sense of emotional and mental clarity, and a stronger desire to be in truth.

During the next year the same basic group and I returned to this place periodically to continue the transformative work we had begun earlier. Each time we would find that by working in our power spots, the energies and secrets of the orishas would be revealed more and more.

Over the course of the year I was able to observe radical changes in my clients' lives. I could give many examples, but two cases come especially to mind. A woman I'll call Caterina was trapped in a marriage with a very domineering man. Although she had wanted to be free of this marriage for years — and worked on it extensively during her sessions — she had neither the courage nor the strength to end it. After she got in touch with her 'male energy' power spot (described in detail in Chapter 3) she returned to Rio with a clear vision of her divorce. She told her husband that very night that she wanted a divorce, and he left the following morning. After the separation, Caterina began a new career and the direction of her life changed completely.

Ricardo was a frustrated high-school teacher who was actively involved with radical politics. When he first came to me for therapy, he was suicidal and needed to find a new direction in his professional life. During one of our workshops in nature, Ricardo suddenly got in touch — for the first time — with the spiritual dimensions within himself. Parallel to this shift in consciousness, he became aware of his interest in a career as a therapist. Over the following year his spiritual awareness continued to expand. He stopped teaching, he left politics, and he is now an excellent therapist incorporating the spiritual dynamic into his work. While Ricardo's initial reactions to being in his power spot were not as dynamic as Caterina's, the way he changed the direction of his life in time was even more substantial.

As we continued with the workshops, I found the direction of my own life changing as well. My new interest in nature powers and nature beings led me to Paulinho, a 'pai de santo' or Candomblé priest. He became my teacher and began to reveal the hidden knowledge and mythology about Candomblé and its close association with the orishas.

This awareness deepened my own inner search and transformed my role as a therapist. From the time of my graduating from medical school, I was fascinated by the psychosomatic aspects of health, and how our feelings, thoughts and emotions help determine whether we are healthy or sick. This eventually led me to pursue a post-graduate degree in psychiatry, which I believed at the time would give me knowledge of how the mind works and its role in human psychodynamics.

My psychiatric training consisted primarily of learning about mental disorders and their treatment with medication and psychotherapies involving support, suggestion and persuasion. By observing our patients and following their progress during my training, I realized that they were not really helped through the methods I was taught. Their inner process remained nearly stagnant, and we were not able to reach them on a deep psychological level. I saw that I was lacking a true understanding of their psychodynamics in order to really help them transform their lives.

At this time, I began to experience doubts in my personal life and felt the need to better understand my own psyychodynamics as well. This realization brought me to begin a long process of psychoanalysis, which eventually led to four years of psychoanalytic training. Parallel to this process, I also participated in a self-explorative training programme involving psychodrama and art therapy, which helped me experience aspects of myself which were merely subjects of discussion in psychoanalysis. Nevertheless, I still sensed that a deeper part of me was not reached by these self-transformative processes.

Within several months, however, I was introduced to the work of Alexander Lowen, the founder of bioenergetics. Bioenergetics is a type of therapy which incorporates opening the energetic blocks in the body that are associated with childhood traumas and other early experiences. By locating and removing these energy blocks through special exercises in conjunction with psychological work, Dr Lowen found that the individual can reach new levels of self-awareness, personal integration and creative expression. My introduction to bioenergetics was a deeply moving experience, and I soon began training with Dr Lowen. Our association continued over the next two years. This work with Dr Lowen and his associates was a turning point in my life. I realized that by working with and transforming the energy blocks in the body, I was able to deal with and transform the psychological issues in my life that I had been working on for so long.

At about the same time, I also began training with Theda Basso, a bodywork therapist in Rio de Janeiro. Through massage and exercise, she helps people open up the energy centres of the body (known as *chakras* in the East). My work with Theda was often dramatic and powerful. It led me to discover spheres of consciousness that went beyond the psychological level and into what mystics have called cosmic or spiritual consciousness. I gradually began to see the world from a more detached yet integrated perspective, and became more aware of spheres of existence that went beyond the physical, emotional of psychological.

While training with Theda Basso, I was also able to begin to experience points within my body (which I later called 'inner power spots') which contained an intense concentration of vibrating energy. By activating these power centres through massage, exercise and breathing techniques, I found that new inner levels of energetic, psychological and mental awareness could be discovered. Through this work with inner power spots, I began to sense — for the first time — the reality of subtler realms of existence. In addition, I began to sense that I was finally arriving at the discovery of my true nature as an integrated and spiritual human being.

Our country workshop took place shortly after I had completed this stage of my psychological work. The discovery of the outer spots and the orishas was greatly to expand and deepen the nature of my work as a therapist, seeker and healer.

During the workshop at Visconde de Mauá, I realized that if we could combine our work on the inner power spots with work involving the outer power spots in nature, new and exciting doors to expanded consciousness could be opened within ourselves. As a result, deep healing and personal transformation could then take place. This vision was confirmed during future workshops.

When I look back over the years of my work and study, I can see the longing to discover my true self. Working to open up new levels of consciousness and trying to resolve the psychological traps I got myself into as a child enabled me to help others to do the same with their own lives.

This path is one of the many paths of self-transformation. For those who identify with this path, I hope that this book can provide some of the tools needed to help you on your journey. Of course, any path that seriously intends to break old psychological patterns and to help us reach our true nature is not always an easy one. However, working on these issues is the only way to reach self-awareness, deep joy and integration in our lives.

This book will be divided into three parts. The following three chapters will examine the nature of true power, which comes from the integration of man and nature. We will also explore the psychological and physical aspects of 'grounding our energy' and learning how to build a solid foundation for working consciously with the forces of the Earth. We will also explore the reality of nature beings and how they relate to power spots on both inner and outer levels.

The second section will focus on the practical methods I have developed to help us make contact with these nature beings. In addition to integrating bodywork, prayer, meditation and conceptual work, we will offer step by step instructions for finding both our inner and outer power spots.

The final section will show how we can integrate our inner powers with the forces of nature around us. This union of the 'inner' and the 'outer' can lay the foundation for important psychological and spiritual growth. It can, in short, help us claim our true power and enable us to walk on the Earth Mother with a sense of clarity, strength and purpose.

José Alberto Rosa, M.D.

Chapter 1

TOWARDS THE
PATH OF POWER

A power spot is a place found in the body and in nature that contains a particularly high concentration of vibrating energy. Each of us has three primary *inner power spots* that are found at the base of the spine, the solar plexus, and near the heart. *Outer power spots* correspond with specific forms in nature, including streams, lakes, mountains and caves.

Why should a person work with power spots? By working with our inner and outer power spots, we can reclaim our lost connection with nature. Because we combine the forces of the 'inner' with the 'outer' we begin to deepen our contact with the environment around us and become more sensitive to the other forms of life it contains. We are also able to perceive the powers of nature that resonate with these physical forms. As a result, we feel more secure and inwardly calm as we feel ourselves as an integrated part of nature rather than an adversary or unwelcome guest.

Working organically with our power spots leads to a degree of emotional and mental clarity that enables us to deal more efficiently with practical issues of life which require our attention. Personal matters concerning health, career, relationship and sexuality can be explored, worked on and resolved from a place of true inner strength.

But more importantly, working with our inner and outer power spots on a regular basis enables us to intensify both the energy and focus needed to deepen and expand our consciousness. This not only leads us to see the truth about our lives, but helps us mobilize the courage we need to deal with often difficult and painful aspects of our personality which need to be transformed. We are able to see the direction of our lives more clearly and to recognize what has prevented us from reaching our full potential. We begin to understand the emotional and mental distortions that have kept us from experiencing real contact with ourselves and others.

As this inner work progresses, we are able to perceive other realms of existence. This leads us to a deeper understanding of the nature of reality. Being in our power spots helps us reach the core of our being.

Pursuing this contact with the subtle realms of nature by working in our power spots can, in time, change our perception of the world around us. Eventually we can discover our real place in the scheme of things and appreciate our small yet significant role in the process of the evolution of the human family.

However, in order to co-operate with the forces of nature on an ongoing basis, a strong personal foundation of inner reality needs to be built. When we wish to expand our consciousness by getting in touch with the subtle realms of existence, we need first to become very familiar with ourselves. This will not only ensure that we will be able to better understand the information we will discover, but will also prepare us to use it in a responsible manner.

The first area of responsibility involves *self-knowledge.* This means being aware not only of our weaknesses (many people actually make a 'career' out of exploiting their weaknesses) but also becoming conscious of our strengths. Many of us have perceived our creative potential, an ability to heal, or a particular talent that could bring us joy and personal fulfilment. Instead, we often spend our lives acting out our weaknesses and creating vicious circles and patterns of disharmony in daily life.

For example, a person may be romantically involved with a variety of partners over the years, but the dynamics of each relationship are invariably the same. The tendency is to blame the world or to lament our bad luck. In contrast, a responsible journey of self-knowledge would involve going within and finding the cause of this repetitive pattern and why we continue to create it.

The second area is *self-responsibility.* The more we work on ourselves, the more we see how we create and re-create (as well as attract) whatever happens in our life.

We perceive that things do not happen by chance. What we call 'chance' is, in reality, a resonance with hidden aspects within ourselves.

We all know people who are repeatedly involved in accidents, robberies, or other violent or unhealthy situations. By working on themselves, they will invariably come into contact with an inner pattern of repressed violence and destructiveness. By becoming aware of these patterns, they are taking responsiblity for these often hidden aspects of their nature. As a result, they are better able to break the old patterns so new ways of interaction can come into play.

Another common human trait is to project our own negative aspects onto others. We blame them, for example, for being jealous, greedy, afraid or angry. When we blame another, we sometimes have a 'charge' or a strong negative reaction towards the particular person or trait. When this happens, it is important that we look at ourselves to find the same aspect within our own nature. This realization can lead us to take responsibility for these aspects instead of projecting them onto someone else.

Humility is the third requirement for the building of a strong inner reality. In our society, we all function with a belief in our own self-importance. This belief inevitably leads to competition, envy, greed and comparison. We are taught to get ahead, to be first, to be more clever or more beautiful, and to strive for more wealth and more influence than our neighbour has. We often associate these things with power, and many people spend their entire lives trying to achieve and maintain them.

As we travel on the path of inner exploration, sooner or later we realize that these attitudes create unhappiness, destructiveness, despair and isolation. Knowing who we are and taking responsibility for our lives leads us little by little to a more accurate perspective of ourselves in the world and in the scheme of things. After a while, we begin to come upon the true meaning of humility, which is an essential step on the path of power.

Honest humility should not be confused with the mask of humbleness which people use to hide feelings of arrogance and self-importance. Rather, true humility comes from a clear perception that we are each but a cell in the body of humanity. Knowing this, I then understand the task of the cell that I am and can function in a way that is in harmony with the laws of that body.

This leads to an understanding of the true meaning and source of power. As we observed earlier, we admire certain qualities, such as competitiveness, the ability to manipulate, greed and aggression, as valuable manifestations of power. In reality, they are distorted reflections of true power.

Power permeates the entire universe. It manifests as the magnetic force that keeps the planets in alignment, and makes flowers grow here on earth. It is the force that stands behind all movement and unfoldment. Without this power, health, harmony and balance would not exist. It is the force behind the light of truth and reaches us through all selfless acts of love.

As human beings, we have a special task regarding this power. Our goal is to channel this impersonal energy and apply it in our daily lives. We can channel this force through the false perception of self-importance and use it for selfish and destructive purposes. Or, power can be channelled through the real self which is grounded in love. Instead of being used for greed, competition or gaining control over others, the real self channels the powers of the universe to protect others and to promote harmony, co-operation and truth on Earth.

Depending on the level of spiritual evolution, as well as our innate talents, education and interests, power can take many different forms. Some of us can manifest it through art, others through physical or emotional healing, while others channel this energy in areas of leadership, science or education. However, these expressions are all reflections of Divine Power and are not connected with personal or self-orientated goals.

The fourth personal quality with which we are concerned involves *communion with the land.* Ancient American indian traditions teach that we are children of both heaven and earth. Because our mother is 'Earth' we cannot receive Father's (Heaven's) strength without being in true contact with our Earth Mother or the land. In addition, in order to receive Father's strength, we not only need to return to the Earth Mother, but also need to reach that 'earthy' quality within ourselves. In psychology this is known as *grounding*.

The concept of walking in balance with the Earth Mother is an essential part of the American indian tradition. Respect for the four kingdoms: mineral, plant, animal and human — is taught to native children even before they are able to walk. In addition, a deep understanding of the 'spirit keepers' of the four elements — air, water, earth and fire — as well as nature beings at other levels of existence make up the foundation of native teachings throughout the Americas. In addition to indigenous teachings, travellers from other lands brought their own traditions to the Americas. In Brazil, for instance, a religion known today as Candomblé, that works with the energies of nature, was brought over from Africa by slaves during the sixteenth century.

At our present moment in human history, the need for alignment with the Earth Mother is especially great. Modern Western civilization is systematically destroying the earth. Streams, rivers, forests, deserts and grasslands are under constant threat from pollution, soil erosion and other forms of attack for short-term financial gain.

As individuals, we follow a similar pattern of alienation from the earth. In order to satisfy personal whim, we often treat nature without respect. Blood sports are perhaps the most obvious example of our insensitivity towards nature, as we kill many thousands of animals for pleasure. However, even when we take a simple walk in the country, we often break tree branches or pick flowers without compunction, forgetting that other life forms deserve a complete life cycle as much as we do.

We also frequently take more from nature than we really need, as evidenced by our excessive personal consumption of food, paper, petrol and wood. Many products (from cars to radios to clothing) are often thrown away rather than being repaired or recycled. Swamps, fields and shorelines become dumping grounds for our garbage. Native teachers feel that the imbalances this abuse creates on all levels of nature — both seen and unseen — expose the entire planet to the threat of extinction.

The human family in particular is passing through a time of dramatic changes. We have all felt the pressure during the last several decades for the transformation of consciousness. The values of ten years ago no longer have meaning as the destruction of old patterns is continuing on a seemingly daily basis. Only those capable of being integrated, both within themselves and with the Earth Mother, will be able to move safely through the times of planetary change and thus help ensure the survival of the earth.

Working with nature spirits or orishas is an important aspect of being in harmony with the Earth Mother. In the first place, we avail ourselves of the subtle forces in nature which can further our own evolution. Orishas not only help our gardens grow better (as well documented by the Findhorn community in Scotland) but, by lending us their energy, can protect us from harm, increase our ability to meditate, and further the healing process on physical, emotional and mental levels. In addition, they can help us get in touch with our 'natural' consciousness and our own inner wisdom. By communicating with these forces in our power spots, we can also co-operate in helping to protect this planet. Through prayer and creative visualization, we can help direct the benign energies of the orishas to further the 'will-to-good' of those humans who are working to promote peace, co-operation and brotherhood.

However, since communication with these forces comes from within, our need to really know ourselves is especially important. In the following chapter, we will explore the psychological aspects of self-awareness and personal grounding. This will help us lay a strong and lasting foundation for the important transformative work we will do in our power spots.

Chapter 2

GROUNDING:
PATH TO THE TRUE SELF

We are each an expression of mind, body and spirit. All three aspects are intimately connected with each other, and have the potential to work together as the foundation for our spiritual growth.

Health is the natural result of these three aspects working together in perfect balance and harmony. Being healthy not only implies the absence of physical or mental illness. A truly healthy individual is able to achieve flowing, full and dynamic contact with the world around him on emotional, mental and physical levels. A healthy person not only can experience a harmonious relationship with others, but also enjoys deep contact within himself and his natural environment. Such a person is deeply rooted to the earth.

HUMAN BODIES

In order to achieve a state of health, we need to maintain the physical body in good condition. As 'the horse on which we ride', the physical body is the temple of our spirit, thoughts and emotions, and requires our ongoing attention and care. Proper food, regular exercise and adequate rest lay the foundation for achieving a healthy physical body. At the present time there are hundreds of good books on the market devoted to its proper culture and care which can be consulted for further study.

In addition to the dense physical body made up of organs, blood, muscle and bone, metaphysicians and scientists teach that we also possess a second, more subtle body, known as the *vital field* or *etheric body.* Composed of streams of vibrating energy, the etheric body penetrates every cell of our physical body. The etheric body provides energy or *prâna* to the physical body and governs the functioning of both our brain and nervous system. Clairvoyants first described the etheric body as a silvery haze extending a few inches beyond the skin. More recently, Kirlian photography has shown it as a vibrating envelope of multi-coloured energy surrounding the body. Its emanations are especially strong from the top of the head and in the hands and fingers of healers. While most of us cannot actually see the etheric body, many have felt it. When we experience a 'tingling' sensation of the skin, we are probably perceiving a hightened activity of energy moving through the etheric body.

Because the etheric body and the physical body are so interconnected, physical health depends on the proper balance and integration of the many energy streams in the etheric body. If there is a block of energy in the etheric body (due to emotional, mental or other factors) the physical body, in time, can become affected. And if there is a physical problem (such as a cut, broken bone, cancer or arthritis) the etheric body can be affected at the same time. The ancient oriental science of acupuncture is based, among other things, on the interrelationship between the physical and vital bodies. The acupuncturist works to increase the body's energy flow by unblocking energy channels called *meridians.* By increasing and/or balancing the energy flow from the etheric to certain organs or other body parts, he can promote their physical well-being.

Beyond the etheric is yet another body, which is called the *astral body.* It is the body of the emotions, and is inter-connected with both the etheric and dense physical bodies. A proper exploration of the astral body deserves several volumes. However, we can only briefly explore a few points as they apply to our discussion here.

All of us have experienced a pain or feeling of discomfort in the physical body when we are afraid, sad or angry. By the same token, we also feel physically well when we fall in love, receive a gift, enjoy someone's company, or hear good news. In many cases, we also respond to an emotional situation with our physical body. We may try to avoid feelings of fear by contracting our shoulders. We attempt to avoid feelings of sadness, loneliness or neediness by tightening the chest, or try to repress anger by tensing some muscles of our back. Some try to deal with the fear of 'letting go' during orgasm by contracting the muscles of the pelvis and abdomen.

From our first years of childhood, these habitual body contractions as a response to emotional stimuli slowly build up muscle tensions which eventually become chronic. These chronic tensions are the result of repressed emotions and feelings which we try to deny. Repressing emotions or feelings by subconsciously contracting the muscles can block the flow of etheric energy which may, in time, produce a physical illness or other imbalance.

On the other hand, repression can create secondary emotional expressions that are substitutes for the repressed or denied primary emotions. For example, a child grows up in a family which did not permit displays of emotion or feelings, but encouraged the child to be orderly, rational and intellectual. Over the years, the child can develop chronic neck tension in an attempt to control and suppress natural emotional reactions. Because the neck separates the chest (the home of the feelings) from the head (the seat of the rational mind) the natural flow of energy between them is blocked. This blockage helps maintain a strong concentration of energy in the head at the expense of the person's total being. As a result, the adult cannot express his emotions: he is unable to cry, cannot express love or other 'heart' feelings, and may even be sexually detached. The world is approached from a strictly rational and intellectual (and therefore distorted and incomplete) point of view.

Beyond the astral, we also possess a *mental body*, which is also interconnected with the others. Unlike the emotional, etheric and physical bodies, the aspects of the mental body are twofold in nature: the *lower mental* is connected with rational thought, intellectual activity and imagination, while the *higher mental body** is associated with creativity and intuitive knowledge. Like the other bodies, this twofold mental body plays a major role in health and disease. Our thoughts, mental images and attitudes not only affect our emotional response, but also our level of energy and our ability to overcome adversity. The pioneer work of Dr Carl and Stephanie Simonton with terminal cancer patients is a case in point. By working with meditation, guided imagery, and the confronting of old attitudes, they have been able to help hundreds of people experience remissions of their disease and enjoy years of active, productive living.**

The role of a creative, adaptable and inquiring mind in maintaining overall health was addressed by L. J. Bendit MD and Phoebe Payne Bendit in *The Etheric Body of Man*:

The living entity has to undergo perpetual readjustment and rebalancing if it is to remain healthy. And the focus of this readjustment is essentially in the mind, where there is a tendency for the earth-tuned aspects to contend against the forces of progress and of increasing consciousness by trying to settle down into mental and emotional grooves. If this inertia reflects into the vital etheric field it too fails to keep pace with the passage of time, and illness results.'

In addition, we have still other subtle bodies of more purified, rarified energy which is connected with spiritual realms. Our spiritual nature may be defined as our 'consciousness or sensitivity towards the environment; a sense of connectedness with all parts of the universe'. Being in touch with our spiritual self implies being grounded in our spiritual centre or *core*. This state of grounding implies a total harmony with Nature and with the laws which govern the universe. It is from this centre where true peace, wisdom and deep compassion reside.

While our spiritual bodies are aspects of higher levels of consciousness, our other bodies are more associated with the earthy planes. When we decide to follow the path of self-enlightenment, we need to integrate our spiritual nature with our physical body, emotions and mind rather than to develop the spiritual aspect at the expense

---

*This body has also been referred to as the *causal body* in theosophical literature.
**For additional information, refer to their excellent book *Getting Well Again* (Los Angeles: J. P. Tarcher, 1980).

of the others. This is why there is no possibility of reaching 'heaven' without being rooted on the earth.

This point can be illustrated by most organized religions and cults today. Many of them work with a belief system concerned with heaven, but tend to miss the 'grounding'. The result is a primarily mental, intellectual or rational understanding of dogma, doctrines and beliefs at the expense of a transformation of consciousness that encompasses the entire being.

Ungrounded spirituality opens the door for us to use the name of God to avoid self-responsibility and to relate to God through a neurotic dynamic filled with projections of ourselves. For example, a person feels unfulfilled in his career: instead of working on his inner motivations for being in his particular career, or asking himself why he has not moved in new directions, he projects his frustrations onto God, holding God responsible for his frustration or lack of fulfilment. In psychological terms, he is 'hooked' in the trap of not owning up to his role in creating his situation and not wanting to work to liberate himself from his trap. He refuses to take personal responsibility for his situation. Doing so would bring him in contact with his inner reality, which contains his deep yearnings, hidden talents and the inner authority he needs to follow.

THE DYNAMICS OF GROUNDING

As we mentioned earlier, our physical body is permeated by streams of flowing energy. This energy circulates in two major patterns: one pattern follows a spiral movement which is centered around the spinal column. The other stream of energy flows up towards the head and down towards the feet through *meridians* or channels. According to early Chinese tradition, we possess more than a dozen specialized meridians for transporting this vital energy (called *chi* by the Chinese) throughout the physical body. As mentioned earlier, these meridians are especially known to acupuncturists, whose task is to remove obstacles in the meridians that limit the flow of *chi* to various parts of the physical body.

We say that a person is *grounded* when this vital energy can flow without hindrance from the top of the head through the whole body to the very bottom of the feet. A grounded person — when performing certain physical exercises — is able to experience a vibrational movement throughout the body with a high concentration of energy in the feet. The feet, legs and pelvis feel warm, strong, and very connected to the ground.

The psychological aspect of grounding brings about a deep sense of feeling as though one is a part of the earth and its energy. The person feels that his weight is supported by his feet and as a result feels centered, confident and very secure. Not only is the physical body more relaxed, but the individual is inwardly calm and clear. He is not only conscious of his own emotions and feelings, but is aware of the feelings of others as well.

The mental component of grounding involves thoughts that are clear and focused. The individual is able to appreciate the total dimension of a situation or problem while seeing how it can be dealt with or resolved. Being mentally grounded helps us work equally well both with broad concepts and specific details. In addition to being able to observe the thoughts and feelings within ourselves, we can also achieve a better understanding of the thoughts, feelings and intentionality of other people.

Spiritual grounding is a natural consequence of physical, emotional and mental grounding. When we are grounded on these three levels, we naturally achieve states of more rarified consciousness. We begin to experience — in a concrete and energetic way — our union with God.

It is important to remember that most of us are more grounded in some aspects than others. Yet until we are energetically, emotionally, mentally and spiritually grounded at the same time, we will not achieve full inner harmony and will have difficulty discovering our true essence.

OBSTACLES TO GROUNDING

We mentioned before that from our earliest years we respond to such feelings as fear, anger and pain by tensing certain groups of muscles. In time, these tensions become chronic and eventually lead to what bodywork therapists call *energetic blocks.*

All children want to be accepted and loved. With this in mind, society values certain modes of behaviour which we believe will lead to our being loved and accepted by others. For instance, expressions of hate, pain, fear and 'craziness' are considered negative. In order to be loved and accepted, the child learns how to repress these natural human emotions and to substitute other responses that are considered more acceptable.

For example, since expressions of aggression in a child are considered negative, children are frequently rejected or punished by their parents when they display such behaviour. The child is admonished to be a 'good boy' or a 'good girl', and gradually learns how to be submissive, and how to cultivate the appearance of being pleasant and agreeable. As the child develops, these reactions are incorporated into the personality until they become automatic unconscious responses. In addition to cultivating specific reactions when dealing with others in society, the repression of 'negative' emotions also occurs when any 'negativity' comes up within themselves.

In the development of the personality, this process occurs in many different emotional areas. As a consequence, it creates a multitude of energetic blocks with their physical emotional and mental components. This leads to patterns of behaviour that we find much more acceptable to society, but at a high cost to our integrity and freedom. These patterns develop first in relations with our immediate families and are strengthened and refined in school, in church and with friends. They are further reinforced during our teenage years, when feelings of sexuality arise.

The expression of substitute behaviour that is a product of repressed natural pulsations also creates what we call *masks*.* A mask is a pattern of psychological and energetic blocks that manifests as a stable expression of behaviour that we create in order to be accepted by others (as well as ourselves) according to what we consider negative within us. Masks of kindness, understanding, detachment and concern are among the most common in Western society. Because they are the products of repression and blocked energy — and represent false emotions and thoughts — masks lack spontanaeity and are intuitively perceived by others as deceptive. As long as we believe they work for us, we can maintain them indefinitely, but at tremendous personal cost.

Patterns of repression and substitution learned in childhood create a stagnant way of thinking, reacting and relating to others as well as to ourselves. In reality, these prescribed automatic responses produce vicious circles of behaviour. What were at first creative ways to protect ourselves from negativity can in time become our prisons.

For example, the 'good' child who replaces feelings of aggression with a mask of submission and pleasantness becomes an adult who makes a career out of being agreeable, accommodating and submissive. By repressing his natural aggression, he has also 'thrown out the baby with the bathwater' and has cut himself off from the positive aspects of aggression, such as self-assertion, decisiveness, taking risks, and the ability to fulfil one's desires and goals. Frustration and bitterness permeate his life because he has become imprisoned in his mask. This prison prevents us from flowing freely energetically, psychologically and mentally. Living in the mask self — with its repression, fear and stagnation — keeps us from being grounded and prevents us from being a channel for the free-flowing energy between heaven and earth.

TOWARDS GROUNDING

Only through becoming aware of this repressed mental and emotional material — and gradually opening the energetic blocks in the body through bodywork techniques — can we get in touch with our real, flowing natural selves. To do this, we have to go back and work on the negative material we have repressed for so long and which has directed our defensive behaviour and reactions for so many years. By carefully working through this old material, we can free ourselves from

---

*For further study, consult Dr Lowen's book, *Physical Dynamics of Character Structure* (also published as *The Language of the Body*, New York: Collier Books).

the prisons we have created. We can experience the 'here and now' rather than compulsively recreating the past in our daily life.

Being grounded in the here and now is a result of the intersection between space and time. Space is connected with our horizontal dimension, which encompasses our relationships with others and our interaction with the world around us. Time is connected with our vertical dimension, and encompasses our interaction with our inner world. This vertical dimension is involved with self-awareness, the opening of psychological blocks, and working through false images, destructive attitudes and harmful behaviour patterns. The vertical dimension is our workshop for the transformation of consciousness, and is the major dimension involved when we work with our inner and outer power spots.

By being grounded in our vertical dimension we can gradually transform our relationships. We come upon new and creative ways of facing challenges. We can explore new avenues of personal growth and find our task in life. This process will also increase our understanding of the spiritual dimensions and enable us to become spiritually aware in a natural, integrated way.

There are, of course, many people who follow an inner path who possess an impressive amount of spiritual knowledge. However, they often miss the integration of all levels of being which brings about true spiritual understanding. Because they often avoid dealing with emotional and mental blocks, they are not really grounded. We mentioned before that there can be no heaven without earth. The first gateway to the spiritual realms is our own humanity: the earthy quality within us. This identification with the earth brings about a natural opening of the heart and leads us closer to a state of selfless love and true compassion.

As mentioned earlier, humility is another important aspect of grounding. It helps us recognize that while we may have certain talents and a specific task to fulfil in life, we are still but a cell in the body of humanity.

However, the most exciting aspect of being grounded is to be able to re-establish direct contact with the earth. When a person is physically, psychologically and mentally grounded (even while living in a large city), going into a field or forest and making contact with the Earth Mother can be a very powerful experience. One feels joy, protection and security in the sense of being 'home'. We realize that we have never experienced our connection with the Earth Mother. At the same time, we become aware of the dynamics of society which help keep us in an ungrounded state.

Not only has this ungroundedness cut human society off from nature, but, as in a vicious circle, this alienation has led society to its ungrounded state. When we as a society lose our grounding, our collective energy goes frequently to the rational mind. As mentioned earlier, this rational approach traps us (both individually and collectively) in compulsive patterns involving greed, status, competitiveness, devotion to appearance values, and trying to find substitutes for the security we have lost by not being grounded. The endless accumulation of material goods in pursuit of security not only alientates us further from the Earth Mother (where true security resides) but also leads to a disregard and even contempt towards the four kingdoms of nature which make up our world. The destruction of forests and other land areas for short-term profit, acid rain, soil erosion, air and water pollution, blood sports, nuclear power plants and toxic waste dumps — these are among the most obvious examples of human destruction of the earth. When we attack the Earth Mother in this way, we expose ourselves to Her response, which makes us even *more* afraid and insecure.

During the last century in my native Brazil, vast forests were devastated in the north-eastern part of the country after it was found that hardwood exports to Europe could bring speculators handsome profits. The large scale deforestation eventually altered rainfall patterns, which left the entire region subject to droughts. At the present time, the once lush 'Nordeste' is the poorest region of Brazil, where drought and starvation are commonplace.

In both Europe and the United States, pollution from industry and motor traffic has led to the production of acid rain. At the time of writing, this acid rain is killing entire forests, as well as poisoning numerous lakes.

In the United States, the dumping of toxic wastes from factories and nuclear power plants has led to many of these toxins leaching into the water table of nearby cities and towns, making the drinking water hazardous for human consumption.

Another example involves the destruction of the Amazon rain forest. Known as the 'lungs of the world' because it produces approximately one-third of all the oxygen consumed on this planet, the Amazon basin has been threatened by professional hunters, lumber companies and petroleum multinationals because it is believed that the region contains vast reserves of oil and natural gas.

There are many other examples of how the abuse of the planet by humans has placed the continued survival of our species in jeopardy. For as a growing number of ecologists have noted, we cannot destroy our living environment with impunity. The vicious cycle is apparent: As children, we block ourselves from our real feelings and as a consequence lose our grounding with the Earth. This lack of grounding leads us to feel insecure, which we try to resolve by accumulating material goods and by trying to exercise our dominion over the land. The callous abuse and exploitation which results leads to serious environmental problems, which in turn threaten our very existence. This makes us even more insecure and ungrounded.

Only by coming back to the land, by respecting the Earth Mother and by making peace with Her can we break the dangerous vicious circles which threaten our existence. By becoming truly grounded we are able (both individually and collectively) to transform our society, which is in a state of crisis and disrepair. We can then create new, more natural ways of living that are in harmony with the earth and which will lead to greater security and balance.

There are other, more personal benefits to this newly found contact with the Earth Mother. As we become more grounded on the earth, we can also begin to appreciate aspects of nature we may never have paid attention to before. Subtle changes in weather patterns, the aroma of flowers, the sounds of the forest, the movement of rivers and streams, and the way that sunlight touches a field can bring new meaning to our lives and can lead us to identify with other forms of nature as aspects of a vital and complex living body.

In time, we may be able to feel the presence of the forces which stand behind these physical expressions, which also govern the falling of rain, the ability for plants to grow and adapt, the movement of wind and water, and the laws which govern thunder and lightning. We slowly begin to realize that the physical world is but one aspect of existence, and that there is also a vast, complex and exciting world beyond the five senses that is waiting to be discovered.

By exploring this world with care and commitment, we can make contact with its inhabitants through special places on earth known as 'power spots'. In the following chapters we will explore these places in nature and the forces which resonate with them. In addition, we will reveal how we can achieve the process of grounding so that we can effectively work with these forces for the expansion of consciousness and the integration of our total self.

Chapter 3

POWERS OF NATURE AND CANDOMBLÉ

When we take a walk in nature, we are able to observe an astonishing variety of forms. Our walk can take us over hills and valleys, through rich meadows covered with wild flowers, or under the shadow of high cliffs. We may ford streams, cool our feet in a mountain lake, or feel the icy spray of a waterfall. Our journey may take us through deep forests, where we can come upon birds, deer, snakes or foxes. By walking silently and with receptive awareness, we can feel our connection to these myriad forms and experience our oneness with them.

During this walk, we can also perceive various sensations as we come upon different aspects of nature that go beyond the five senses. We can feel a different energy when we stand in a meadow to the energy we feel when we are sitting on top of a mountain. A stream gives us a different feeling to a lake. We perceive a different energy emanating from a large outcrop of rocks to that which flows from a majestic grove of trees. Each of these natural forms has its own vibration. When we move among them we are not only perceiving different forms of physical manifestation (like rivers, trees and rocks) but are also perceiving the subtle realms of existence that are connected with these forms. This is the realm of existence inhabited by what are known as nature spirits, devas ('shining ones') or *orishas*. It is this realm of existence which we are addressing in this book.

Every native culture has worked in one way or another with nature beings. In addition to acknowledging their connection with the elements of fire, water, air and earth, anthropological evidence regarding ancient cultures throughout the world abounds with references to sacred and ceremonial places, including mountains, lakes, waterfalls and rivers. To these native peoples, the energy beings connected with these places were as real as the rivers and rocks themselves. This special relationship between humans and nature spirits was a central part of their lives. They knew that the major task of the devic beings was twofold: first, to stand behind the evolution of all physical forms on Earth; and secondly, to aid in the upliftment of humanity. These people were aware that nature beings could share — on subtle levels — the wisdom, hope and healing that was essential to human development and growth.

As modern civilization began to create towns and cities, most of humanity has, over the centuries, gradually lost contact with the earth. As a consequence, it has also lost contact with these subtle forces in nature. By doing this, we have cut ourselves off from an important source of guidance, wisdom and healing, which can teach us how to live in harmony with the Earth Mother, with ourselves, and with every one of Her children.

Fortunately, some of the early traditions that were deeply involved with the subtle forces in nature still survive today. One of them is known as *Candomblé*. Brought from Africa (primarily from what is today Nigeria, Angola and the Congo) to the shores of Brazil by slaves in the sixteenth century, the religion of Candomblé is currently practised by millions of people. Most of the Brazilian devotees of Candomblé live in the northern coastal cities of the country, including São Salvador, Belém, Fortaleza and Rio de Janeiro. Although we may not agree with or relate to some of the rituals of Candomblé as practised today, we can benefit from Candomblé's unique teachings which describe the characteristics of these nature beings and show how to communicate with them.

According to Candomblé tradition, there is an all-powerful and all-encompassing God, called *Olorun,* who created the heavens and earth. Olorun also created all the myriad forms of life who inhabit both the seen and unseen worlds on this planet. Unlike Christian theology which believes in a personal God, Candomblé views Olorun as a benign yet impersonal force. For this reason, He created an army of helpers in the unseen worlds who exist not only to assist in the evolution of nature, but also to provide personal assistance and support to the human members of Olorun's vast family. These beings, which never take physical forms, are known both in Africa and Brazil as *orishas.*

Like other religious philosophies, Candomblé speaks of the inherent dualism in creation, and that *yin* and *yang* energies are inherent in every life form. For this reason, Candomblé teaches that there are both male and female orishas.

According to Candomblé, we receive both a 'father' and a 'mother' orisha when we are born. The task of these devic 'parents' is to provide us with protection and guidance during our evolutionary journey on earth. Each orisha is connected with a specific element in nature. In order to discover our father and mother orishas, we need to discover the elements with which we best resonate in nature. The places in nature where these elements predominate (and where we feel the strongest resonance) are called our *personal outer power spots.* For that reason, each of us has a 'male' and a 'female' power spot in nature. The connection between our orishas and our power spots is obvious: our power spot is the earthy home of our orisha. It is in this home where we can receive the fullest measure of the orisha's benign strength, wisdom and healing.

Orishas are believed to be related to each other like different members of a family. In addition to being the subjects of a multitude of stories and myths, each orisha is said to possess unique psychological characteristics which set it apart from the others. According to African tradition, there are some four hundred different orishas, but many are not connected with actual power spots. In the following pages we will examine the family of the major orishas that are connected with power spots, and will discuss the personal characteristics of each.

OSHALA (Oxalá)

Oshala is considered the father of all the orishas and the grandfather of all mortals. As an extremely powerful nature being, He resonates with the energy of mountaintops, along with the vast expanses of sky which surround them. Oshala is said to be androgynous, and symbolizes the male and female qualities of nature as well as both the creative and procreative aspects of the universe. On a psychological level, He represents justice tempered by love, as well as the purifying aspect of conscious awareness.

In Brazil, Oshala is compared to Jesus Christ or Nosso Senhor do Bomfin de Salvador da Bahia. Because His favourite colour is white, He is said to resonate well with white metals, such as aluminium, silver and white gold. His consecrated day is Friday.

YEMANJÁ (Iemanjá)

Yemanjá is known both in Africa and Brazil as the 'mother' of all the orishas, and is compared to Our Lady of Conception in the Roman Catholic Church. Her domain includes the oceans and all bodies of salt water, and She is among the most popular and revered of the orishas in Brazil. Yemanjá represents the maternal forces of nature, and is often characterized as a beautiful and exalted figure of spiritual motherhood, coming forth out of the sea dressed in flowing light blue robes. Although She is considered a peaceful, serene nature being, Yemanjá can also be emotionally unstable, with a strong temper and an unforgiving nature. Her colours are white, light blue and silver, and She likes sea stones, shells, white roses and perfume. Yemanjá's day of worship is Saturday, when thousands of Brazilians go to the shore to pay homage to Her.

NANAN (Nanã)

Legend has it that Nanan is the oldest of the orishas, and is affectionately called *vovó* or 'grandmother' by Her devotees. Known variously as the wife or lover of Oshala and the mother of Omolu (the orisha of healers), She corresponds with the energy of St Anne in the Catholic religion, who is the mother of the Virgin Mary.

Nanan is the orisha of still, fresh waters, and Her domain includes still lakes, marshes and swamps. Clay and mud are Her elements, and white and dark blue are believed to be Nanan's favourite colours.

She is often viewed as a wise old woman, who dances with dignity. Nanan is said to be calm, calculating and stubborn, and is deeply connected to domestic life. Her consecrated days are Saturday and Monday.

OSHUNMARÉ (Oxunmaré)

Oshunmaré is the orisha of rainbows and is responsible for the communication between the superior and inferior cosmic regions. Known also as *Rongorô*, He is said to be the son of Yemanjá and the servant of Shangó. Traditional teachings claim that Oshunmaré is bisexual and represents the integration of both male and female aspects of nature. His preferred colours encompass all seven colours of the rainbow. Tuesday is the day the Candomblé priests set aside to honour Oshunmaré. It is believed that Rongorô's movements are like those of a snake, whose undulations reveal the link between heaven and earth. He is associated with St Bartholomew.

SHANGÓ (Xangô)

Shangó is one of the most popular orishas, and is called 'The King of Justice' by His followers. He is the orisha of thunder, and resonates with the energy of storms, caves and large rocks. Often compared to St Jerome, Shangó is seen as the force which makes for justice and wisdom, prosperity and peace. He is also viewed as 'The Master of Fire'.

Originally considered to be a hermaphrodite, Shangó's present image is basically masculine. He is 'married' to Yansan, the orisha of winds, and is also considered to be an amorous adventurer and fierce warrior. On a psychological level, Shangó is said to possess an explosive temper but can also be kind and very reserved. His devotees wear white and red, and His consecrated day is Wednesday. Copper is Shangó's earth element.

OSHOUN (Oxúm)

Oshoun is the orisha of flowing fresh waters and can be found primarily by rivers, waterfalls, springs and streams. She is often viewed as the earthy aspect of motherhood as opposed to Yemanjá, who represents its spiritual aspect. As a wife of Shangó (as well as a former wife of Oshossi, the orisha of forests), Oshoun is connected to romantic love, marriage and human fertility. She is also the Goddess of Prosperity, and is believed to bring material wealth to Her human children.

Candomblé mythology describes Oshoun as a coquettish and vain orisha who likes jewellery, perfume and elegant clothes. Despite these attributes, however, Oshoun is identified with the Virgin Mary in Roman Catholic tradition. Oshoun's consecrated day is Saturday, and Her colour is Yellow. As can be expected, Oshoun's preferred metals are yellow in colour, such as bronze and gold.

OMOLU (Omulú)

Omolu is perhaps the most respected of the orishas, for He is believed to have control over the powers of life and death. Originally connected with agriculture, Omolu is presently known as the orisha of contagious diseases with the ability both to begin and to stop epidemics. Considered 'The Doctor of the Poor' along the Brazilian coast, Omolu has often been identified with St Lazarus the healer.

Omolu is found primarily in green meadows and His power is connected with the energy produced when sunlight touches the surface of a meadow or field. Because He is the orisha of life and death, the beginning of the day (when the sun is rising) is considered the time of ascending life. The middle of the day (when the sun is the strongest) is seen as the transition point between life and death, while the descending sun is connected with death. For this reason, people are cautioned to work with Omolu only in the morning and *never* after the noon hour.

Despite His connection with death, Omolu is viewed as a generous, kind and nurturing orisha. The act of healing invokes the presence of Omolu, and all healers are said to enjoy His protection and guidance. Omolu's principal colours are maroon, white and black, and Monday is His day of worship.

OSHOSSI (Oxossi)

Oshossi is the orisha of the woods and the jungle, and Candomblé tradition describes Him dwelling in an impenetrable forest surrounded by wild animals. Oshossi is, above all, 'the great hunter' (His symbol is the bow and arrow) and is the protector of hunters. As a husband (or, some say, the former husband) of Oshoun, Oshossi is connected to the healing powers of medicinal plants. In Catholic tradition, He corresponds with the energy of St Sebastian.

Oshossi has been described as an extremely active nature being, who never rests. He is seen as clever, quick and always alert, with the tendency to be emotionally unstable. The colours worn by devotees of Oshossi are blue, green or a combination of both. He is said to be very fond of corn and wine, and His favourite metal is bronze. Thursday is the day that is consecrated to Oshossi.

OGOUN (Ogun)

The image of Ogoun is the same as that of St George killing the dragon. He is the orisha of war, and is said to protect his devotees from enemies and danger. Because He is closely associated with iron, Ogoun is also the orisha of agriculture and is the patron of farmers, blacksmiths and others who work with iron implements. Candomblé teachings also describe Ogoun as the God of Surgery, who also oversees the work of dentists. In addition, Ogoun is believed to be connected with any enterprise involving iron, such as architecture, mining and engineering. Because Ogoun is also the orisha of roads, (in Candomblé tradition He is responsible for opening the crossroads so that other orishas can attend ceremonies), He is also considered the patron of the motor car and the train.

Ogoun is said to be romantically linked with both Oshoun and Yansan in Candomblé lore, and is believed to reside in dense forests near veins and outcroppings of iron. Although Ogoun dwells in the domain of Oshossi, His presence can be determined through intuition, as His energy is more aggressive and warlike than that of Oshossi. The children of Ogoun wear dark blue and have consecrated Tuesday as His day of worship.

When we make contact with orishas, we also get in touch with other inhabitants of the subtle realms of existence. As on the earth plane, the subtle realms of nature are inhabited by a tremendous variety of living forms. And like the evolution of life on the earthly plane, these beings also exist in various stages of evolution in the subtle world. Some of these beings have always been evolving in these subtle planes. Others have incarnated at one time or another in physical forms like animals, trees or human beings, and are continuing their evolution in subtler forms.

In our life, we often know of people who are negative. They lie, they cheat, they are bothersome, and may try to prevent others from progressing on their path. Beings of this nature also exist in the hidden planes, and often try to intimidate, seduce or deceive. Like human beings, they may try to disguise their true nature in order to use us for their own purposes. For this reason, it is not only important to be aware of these beings, but also to understand why we attract them to us. As in the physical world, the adage 'like attracts like' is applicable in the subtle world.

When we sincerely commit ourselves to follow the path of love and truth in our lives, we develop a sense of self-awareness, compassion and humbleness. To the degree that we follow this inner path, we will naturally resonate with similar energies and beings which inhibit the subtler planes of existence. When we meet them, we will intuitively feel their love, support and protection as we progress on our spiritual journey.

In addition, each one of us has individual guides and helpers which exist at different levels of evolution in the subtle realms. For example, we have our male and female orishas, which we have spoken of earlier. Besides this 'father' and 'mother', we have the protection of other orishas who work in the background. They may be more present or more distant, depending on our needs of the moment.

According to theosophical and other esoteric teachings, the subtle world is also inhabited by angels and archangels. They have reached a very high level of evolution in the subtle planes and are considered to be even higher than the orishas. Like our personal orishas, we also receive the protection of a specific angel throughout our life. In the Catholic Church, this angel is called our *Guardian Angel* and comes to our aid during very dangerous or otherwise difficult moments. Although many of us are very eager to learn exactly who our Guardian Angel is, He will reveal Himself only when He feels that we are ready.

Besides these angelic beings, we can also have several *spirit guides* who have incarnated previously and who work with us during our life. In addition, we may have other spirit guides who enter our life at certain times according to a specific need. For example, an author writing a book on a certain aspect of architecture could attract the assistance of a spirit guide with a similar interest who would provide encouragement, offer ideas, and facilitate the locating of new sources of information. If one is following a spiritual path which requires deep personal work, one can attract a spirit guide who can, on subtle levels, offer support, encouragement and insight.

In this chapter we have presented only a brief discussion of the vast and largely indescribable world of the orishas and the other inhabitants of the subtle planes of existence. As your journey progresses, you will open yourself to a wide variety of sights, experiences and relationships which are impossible to describe in a book such as this one.

For this reason, it is important to lay a strong personal foundation to ensure your safe journey into this world and to fully experience and integrate the guidance, healing and teaching that is available there. It is important to remember that the subtle realms have no physical manifestation. In order to make contact with its inhabitants, we need to go within ourselves and to follow the voice of our intuition.

In the following chapter, we will show how to both deepen and expand our consciousness so that we can get in touch with these subtle realms. By discovering and working with our inner power spots, we can create a strong foundation for the important and exciting journey which lies ahead.

Chapter 4

DISCOVERING YOUR INNER POWER SPOTS

Inner power spots are points in the body which contain an intense concentration of vibrating energy. Finding these power spots brings about alignment, clarity and inner strength in addition to releasing blocked energy. The energy released is not only of an etheric nature, but is connected with repressed emotions, thoughts, and images which eventually come into awareness when such blocks open up.

When we contact and work with our inner power spots, we take the first step in an accelerated process of opening ourselves to deeper levels of consciousness. At times, this step can be very difficult and requires extraordinary persistence, honesty and compassion towards oneself. However, little by little we begin to feel ourselves more flowing, more natural, and less likely to attempt to control the world around us. We get more deeply in touch with our emotions, our desires and our full inner being. Essentially, working with our inner power spots develops four important qualities which lay the foundation for a deeper phase of self-exploration and inner discovery:

1. We become grounded. Walking with our feet planted firmly on the ground (both in the literal and figurative sense) we begin to feel true contact with the Earth Mother. We slowly develop a quality of natural simplicity, directness and clarity in our relationships with others and in our ability to deal with the challenges and choices of daily life.
2. We discover humility as the psychological aspect of grounding. Only when we are truly humble are we truly grounded. In contrast, the belief in our own self-importance cuts us off from the pulse of life, and separates us from other people, animals and nature. Humility is an expression of letting go of mental control and helps us gain a true perception of ourselves in relation to the universe.
3. We become more in touch with our sexuality and emotional nature, as well as with our ability to love. When we work with our first inner power spot, we remove sexual blocks and get in touch with our dormant 'animal power' within.
    When we activate the second power spot, we come into contact with an enormous variety of emotions. By bringing these emotions to the surface and

into the light, we can transform their energy into positive tools for integration and forward movement.

When we are open to our third inner power spot, we discover the true meaning of love and compassion. As a result, our relationships reach a new and exciting level of passion and intensity, yet remain free from the jealousy, manipulation and possessiveness that pass for 'love' in the accepted sense.

4. We begin to discover the vertical dimension within us and become a channel for the flowing energies between heaven and earth.

As we described in Chapter 2, the horizontal dimension is connected to communicating with others, working at a job, and relating to the outer world in general. However, many of us spend most of our lives in the horizontal dimension at the expense of not being in contact with the world within us. Instead of working to unfold our true potential (which is, in reality, our true wealth) from where we can express our strength, joy and creativity in the outer world, we deny it. We concentrate our energy on becoming a 'success' in the eyes of others and work primarily to accumulate money, material goods, and the status they bring. Or, we compulsively use our time in the pursuit of stimulation through television, going to bars and pubs, or being entertained through certain books, movies or spectator sports. As a consequence, we live on the periphery and rarely give ourselves the opportunity to make deeper contact with our inner or vertical dimension.

We could symbolize the vertical dimension by drawing an imaginary line from the centre of the very top of the head down through the body to the middle of the perineum. If we spread our feet apart to shoulder width, the line would end on the ground at a point equidistant from both feet, as seen in figure 4.1.

It is from this vertical dimension that we are able to get in touch with higher levels of consciousness. As we see, we have one point reaching skyward (heaven or father principle) and one point reaching the ground (earth or mother principle). This is a physical expression of our relationship between heaven and earth.

There are three primary inner power spots in the body and they are found along this vertical axis we have just described. The first inner power spot is located in the perineum. In women, it is located at the posterior angle of the vulva (labia majora) and in men, midway between the scrotum and the anus. It is the centre of our vital force and is connected to our sexuality. This is also the centre that connects us to the ground through the legs; it anchors us to the earth and enables us to develop the quality of groundedness so necessary for integration and balance. If we were to imagine ourselves as a tree, the first power spot would be the base of the trunk and our legs would be the roots, reaching deep into the ground. For this reason, this power spot is the basis for our strength, balance and stability.

This power spot is also connected with our 'primary instinctual force' or *animal power*. It is the remaining link we have with our early animal ancestors. As opposed to societal conditioning and educated intelligence, our animal power brings out our survival instinct, our innate intelligence, and the perceptive awareness we need to make major life decisions.

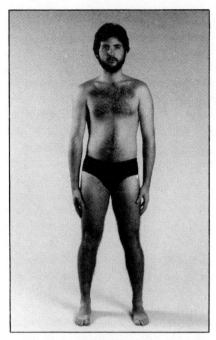

Figure 4.1

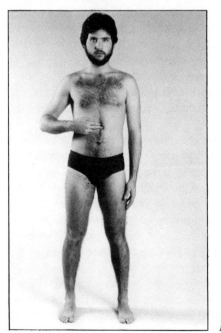

Figure 4.2

The second primary power spot is located at the solar plexus, as shown in figure 4.2. It is connected with the world of personal attachment and brings us in contact with emotions of dependency, jealousy, possessiveness, fear and competitiveness. On a more positive note, it is also the centre of our individual power and contains the force behind our wanting to get a job, feed our families, create a niche in the world and strive for our personal fulfilment.

In other words, the solar plexus is the centre of our personality, and the unique characteristics that make us human. In esoteric language, it is the power spot connected with the astral level of our being. While living in this centre can be very exciting, it can also create much pain. This pain is due primarily to our emotions of attachment and our inability to view an issue or problem in a clear and detached way.

By contacting and opening up this power spot, we can get in touch with material that relates to the world of the personality. When we become aware of and work with 'what we have in us' — and the price we pay for choosing to attach ourselves to emotions of jealousy, competitiveness and so on — we are able to disengage ourselves gradually from the world of attachment. Then we begin to transform these negative patterns and progressively discover, little by little, the world of love and compassion. However, many spiritually orientated people unconsciously misuse this basic truth by repressing the negative feelings in order to reach higher levels of consciousness. Because this 'negative' material is not recognized, they are not able to attain a truly grounded spirituality.

The third power spot is located in the middle of the chest, as seen in figure 4.3. If we draw an imaginary line through the middle of the sternum, we will locate this important power spot in ourselves.

This power spot is connected with love. In its pure and radiant state, this centre is capable of pouring out forces of deep compassion, respect and caring, asking nothing in return. It contains the seed of intuitive knowledge and spiritual awakening.

We mentioned earlier that the second power spot is related to issues of personal love. Through an ongoing process of self-awareness and the transformation of the emotional material connected with the second power spot, we can purify the emotions — like dependency, longing and craving — into a state of self-acceptance and self-love. When we begin to reach the world of self-love, we are able to start letting go of craving, longing and possessiveness and come upon, little by little, a state of universal love and true compassion. Needless to say, this is a long and often difficult process, but it is a necessary part of our path of unfoldment and spiritual awakening.

If issues of personal love of the second power spot are not yet transformed, the opening of the heart centre can not only prolong emotions of longing, craving and dependency, but can also increase the danger of physical illness. Heart palpitations, angina or even heart attack can result when this centre is prematurely opened without

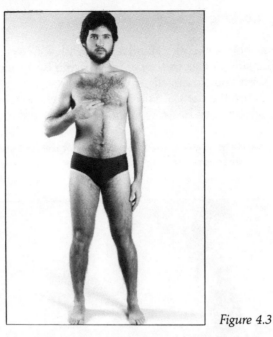

Figure 4.3

a knowledgeable guide to aid in this process of accelerated self-development and self-discovery.

There are other power spots that can be reached after much work and self-purification. However, at the point of having opened the three major power spots just described, a deep level of intuitive wisdom will profuse your entire being. The more we know about who we are, the more we integrate heaven and earth within us. As this process gradually unfolds, other power spots will naturally be discovered. The heart centre is the opening door to the other spiritual dimensions connected to other power spots in the body. In the following pages we will show how we can discover and safely work with our three primary inner power spots and lay the foundation for grounded spiritual work.

Grounding is the primary step in the process for opening our inner power spots.

Exercise 1. Rocking

Remove your shoes and socks, stand relaxed with your feet apart to shoulder width, hands at your sides. Relax the upper part of your body, including shoulders, neck and arms. Keep your knees slightly bent.

Gently rock on the balls of your feet until you are standing on your toes, and then rock back on your heels. Continue this back and forward rock for three to five minutes.

This exercise is designed to increase contact of the feet and ankles with the earth. While you can perform this exercise anywhere, it is better to do so outdoors on the grass.

Exercise 2. Knee Bending

With both feet on the ground and your weight on the balls of your feet, gently bend your knees while exhaling. Then straighten up again while inhaling slowly. Do not lock your knees when you straighten up. Continue this exercise in slow motion for three to five minutes.

This exercise will help open up the energy blocks in the legs and feet, and increase the flow of energy through the legs, thighs and feet.

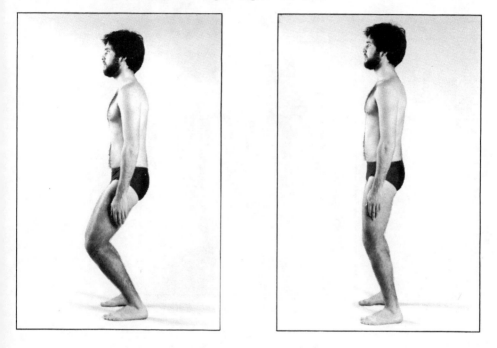

Exercise 3. Shaking

Shake out your legs, one at a time, for five to ten seconds. The feet should be involved with this exercise as well. Repeat five times for each leg and foot. This exercise is designed primarily to release energy.

Exercise 4. Deep Knee Bends

Stand with your feet apart. While keeping your feet on the ground, move into a squatting position, with the arms and hands pointing forward for balance. Move up and down approximately eighteen times per minute for a total of thirty to sixty deep knee bends.

Use this exercise to increase the energy in the legs and thighs. When you complete this exercise, repeat exercise 3.

Exercise 5. Foot Stretch

In a squatting position, place your arms inside your knees with your hands flat on the floor before you. You will be naturally balanced on the balls of your feet. Slowly rock forward and press on your outer four toes. Then rock back slowly, standing up slightly until you feel that you are balanced primarily on your heels.

Place your arms outside your knees, with both hands on the floor. This time, place your weight on your big toe and stretch.

Repeat this exercise several times. It will stretch the muscles of your feet with special emphasis on the toes and heel.

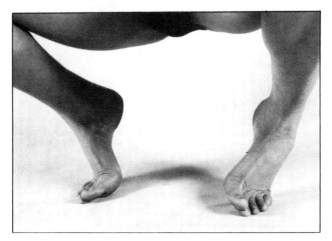

Exercise 6. 'Slalom'

Standing with your legs slightly bent to the left, place your weight on the outer edge of your left foot and the inner edge of your right foot. When you feel as though you have had a good stretch, reverse positions. Repeat five to ten times.

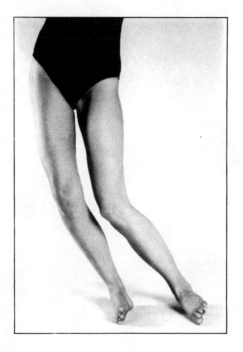

Exercise 7. Foot Contraction

From a standing position with knees slightly bent, place one foot before the other and lift it so that it is off the ground. Contract your toes strongly. Then, open the foot and expand the toes as far as they can open. Repeat five times. Reverse to the other foot and repeat the exercise.

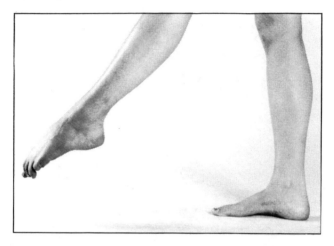

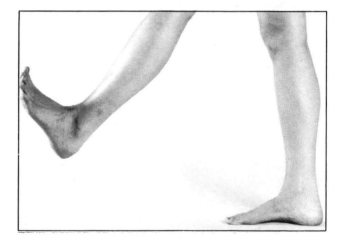

Exercise 8. Leg Stretch 1

Squat down as you did in exercise 4. While in the 'down' position, place your right hand and fingertips behind you and the left hand and fingertips in front. With your right foot on the ground, stretch the left leg to the side. Stretch the left leg three times. Then reverse your position and stretch the right leg. Repeat three times.

Repeat the entire sequence three times.

Now bend down again, but with your left leg extended, and turn to the right. Press and stretch so that the left leg is thoroughly stretched. Move again to the centre position and repeat with the right leg.

Repeat this sequence three times.

Exercise 9. Leg Stretch 2

From the squatting position of the previous exercise, stand up slowly, but keeping your hands on the floor. Without lifting your heels, slowly 'walk' forward with your hands until your legs are completely stretched. Remain in this position for two to three minutes. Then 'walk' back slowly until you return to your original position. Begin to get up slowly by pressing on the balls of your feet.

Repeat exercise 3.

Exercise 10. The Body Shake

Stand up and shake your entire body, making sure that all joints are completely relaxed. Continue this body shake for at least one minute. After the previous exercise, it should be fun.

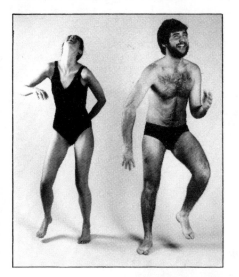 

Exercise 11. Pelvic Circling

Stand up and move your pelvis slowly in the three following ways: back and forth (forward and back); left and right (sideways); in a circular motion.

Continue each exercise segment for at least five minutes.

The goal of this exercise is to energize the pelvis and to release pelvic tension. It is possible that some people may find the exercise uncomfortable because sexual feelings may be felt. If this occurs, try not to repress these feelings, but be sensitive to whatever emotional material comes up.

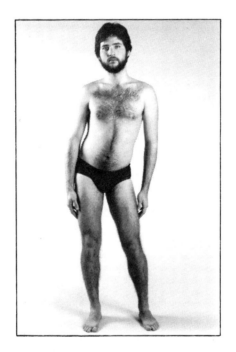

Exercise 12. Grounding 1

This is the famous 'grounding exercise' of Dr Alexander Lowen, the developer of bioenergetics. It is an exercise which you can use any time you need to ground yourself. When you feel ungrounded, or feel as though you are 'holding' energy in your head and shoulders, this exercise can be a valuable friend to help you find your natural self again.

Standing with your feet apart to shoulder width, bend your knees slightly. Placing your weight on the balls of the feet, bend forward and touch the ground with your fingertips. It is not necessary to lean on your fingertips, but merely touch the ground with them. Make sure that your back and neck are completely relaxed. Your toes and heels should be raised slightly off the ground, with your weight on the balls of the feet.

Slowly bend your knees while exhaling gently. Then, *almost* straighten your knees while inhaling, getting into the stretch, with both hands still touching the ground. Continue this exercise for three to five minutes, approximately ten times per minute.

You will probably begin to feel a vibration in the legs as the energy starts to move through them. When this vibration becomes strong, remain in the position with your knees almost straight. Let your legs vibrate and continue to breathe deeply. Remain in this position for several minutes, making sure that your trunk, neck and head are very loose.

Feel if there is any stiffness, cramp or energy blockage in your legs or feet. If so, remain in the bending position and gently hit, with a closed hand, the area of the legs or feet that is blocked. If you have an exercise partner, ask him/her to do this for you in addition to applying a light massage to the arms, shoulders, neck, back or anywhere else you feel tension.

Getting up: with your feet planted firmly on the ground, slowly begin to 'roll' yourself up vertebra by vertebra, while pushing down on the balls of your feet. Allow the vibration in your legs to continue. Take at least forty-five seconds to return to your original standing position, with knees slightly bent as opposed to locked.

Repeat exercise 3, and follow with exercise 10.

Exercise 13. Grounding 2

This is another traditional grounding exercise developed by Dr Lowen.* Stand with your feet apart almost as far as you can spread them, but with toes pointing inward. Try to balance a bit on the outer edge of your feet, while squeezing your knees slightly towards each other.

Your pelvis should be pushed naturally backwards, and your arms should be hanging in front of you. Stay in this stressful position for several minutes, breathing deeply in your belly. You will soon experience an increasing vibration in your legs. Let this vibration continue for five minutes while you continue breathing deeply and slowly.

*For additional exercises developed by Dr Lowen, refer to his book *The Way to Vibrant Health* (see bibliography).

Exercise 14. Pelvic Rock

From the stressful position of the previous exercise, move your feet several inches closer together, and point your toes forward.

Gently rock your pelvis forward slowly, using your thighs rather than tensing the glutus muscles of the buttocks. This rocking motion should be so slow that it is almost imperceptible to an observor. Breathe slowly through your belly. As you slowly rock the pelvis forward and back, be aware of the vibrations you experience, and try to find, while rocking slowly, a specific point where the vibration and energy are the strongest.

Stop when you reach this spot of maximum vibration. It is the place of your first primary power spot.

Exercise 15. Making Inner Contact

Now that you have located your first power spot, you can move your feet closer until they are at shoulder width. However, when you move your feet closer together, try not to lose contact with your first power spot.

You should be standing with your knees almost straight, with an intense vibration moving through your body (and especially the pelvis). Breathe from your belly and be aware of any emotional material that may surface. This may include direct emotions like anger, sadness and sexual excitation, or can include mental images, thoughts and fantasies. Explore this material. Get in touch with your emotions regarding them, so the energy they contain can be released and transformed. For some people, this process can be easy, while others may need more time to work through this emotional material.

When the energy is released and transformed, you will naturally feel that the energy will move upwards through the vertical axis we described at the beginning of this chapter. When you feel this energy moving upwards (reaching the navel and higher) you can perform several exercises to help you find your second primary inner power spot. The following Lowen exercise is designed to help open the area of the solar plexus. This will, in turn, enable us to come into contact with this second major power centre.

Exercise 16. Abdominal Stretch

Stand with your feet apart at shoulder width, and bend your knees slightly. Make fists and place them into the kidney area of the small of your back. Sustain your body on your fists, so that you are leaning your upper body against them. Breathe into your stomach as opposed to breathing through the upper chest.

As a variation, you can raise both arms straight above the head (as opposed to placing your fists into the kidney area) until you are stretching the stomach muscles. Like the previous exercise segment, this variation will open up the solar plexus area and release the energy of the second power spot.

You will soon begin to feel an intense vibration in your solar plexus. Try to stay with this vibration and get in touch with the emotions, images and fantasies which surface at this time. Remain in this position for as long as needed to move through your feelings. Allow these expressions to come out and work with them. In many cases, it is useful to have a partner or the help of an experienced therapist.

When you have completed this exercise, write down your experiences in a notebook. Try to make sense out of this material and see how it relates to your life.

The physical grounding exercises we've described in this chapter (exercises 1-16) should be performed together as a series on a regular basis. As you continue with them, you will probably discover patterns of emotions, thoughts or behaviour that you will want to explore more deeply. The work needed to open the second power spot can take quite a long time. For some people, this process can take several years.

Before we proceed to the third inner power spot, we need to speak briefly about the diaphragm. The diaphragm is a transverse muscle which separates the abdominal cavity from the thorax. On a more subtle level, it also separates the second and third inner power spots. This muscle is often tense and energetically blocked because, for emotional reasons, we prefer the shallow breathing of the upper chest to deep breathing involving both the chest and the belly. When the diaphragm is blocked, the opening of the third power spot is a very difficult process. The previous two exercises (exercises 15 and 16) will help open the diaphragm. Getting in touch with the diaphragmatic block is often very difficult, and may require the help of a bodywork expert.

The opening of the third power spot should occur gradually and naturally. However, there are several exercises designed to release blocked energy in the chest which will help us get in touch with this powerful centre. One of them is a breathing exercise that releases tension in the chest which blocks the energy of this power spot. These tensions are often the result of unresolved fear, longing for love, and loneliness which frequently surface when we work with the second inner power spot. The following exercises should be performed after you have completed the previous sixteen.

Exercise 17. Opening the Chest 1

Stand with your knees slightly bent with your hands clasped behind your buttocks. The thumbs should be pointing towards the floor. Gradually turn the hands together so that the thumbs move in a clockwise direction. The palms of the hands should now be facing downwards. Then raise your arms as high as you can. You will begin to feel pressure on your shoulder blades, and your chest will naturally expand.

Remember that this particular exercise can be extremely powerful and can release very deep feelings.

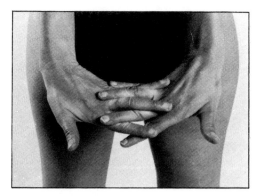

Exercise 18. Opening the Chest 2

This is a less intense variation to the previous exercise. Lay down on your back, knees bent, with your feet on the floor. Place a pillow below your shoulder blades so that your chest naturally expands. Breathe slowly and deeply, and get in touch with any emotions or feelings which may surface.

A Note About Breathing

Working with exercises to help open our inner power spots increases the energy flow of the body. As a result, we become more aware of chronic body tensions we may not have been conscious of before. As we said earlier, these chronic tensions are connected with repressed emotions. We need to be aware of these emotions in order to free ourselves from the constrictions they produce on physical, emotional and mental levels.

As we have seen, one effective way for opening these blocks is through breathing. By utilizing the power of breath, we can consciously direct streams of energy in the body. We can breath through the chest, from the belly, or through a combination of both.

Before you begin, place one hand on your chest and the other hand on your belly. When you breathe through your chest, the hand on your chest should move while the hand on your belly does not. You may feel your shoulders rise and fall and can sense your diaphragm rising. Your belly may pull up slightly. This type of breathing is especially helpful to remove tensions in the upper part of the body. As a result, it allows the emotions behind these blocks to be released.

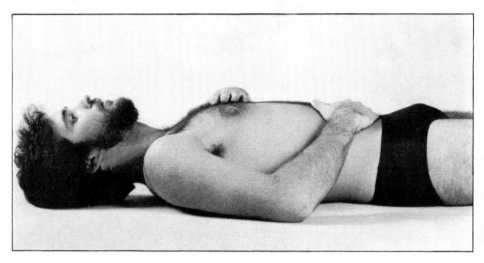

When breathing from your belly, the opposite will occur. When you inhale, your belly will expand while your chest will remain still. Belly breathing releases tensions in the lower part of the body, and is particularly useful for grounding your energy.

Place your index finger just below the sternum. Breathe into this specific point, inhaling through both the chest and the belly. This type of breathing is useful for integrating the upper and lower parts of the body and the emotional responses connected with it.

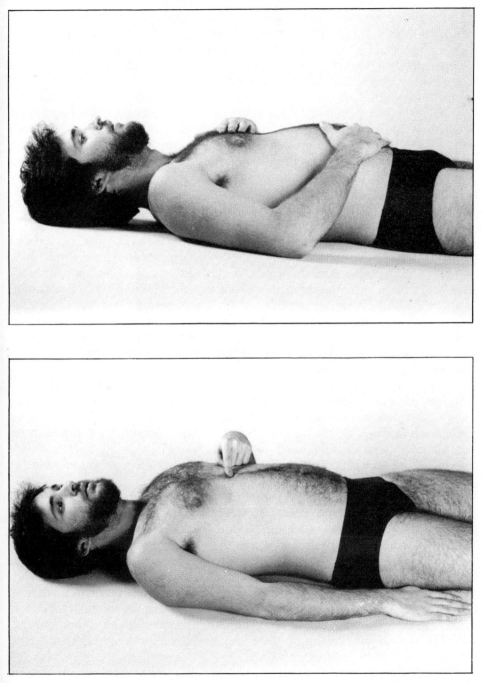

If the tension you wish to work with is in the upper part of the body, use the breathing technique that combines both the chest and the belly. If the tensions are centered in the lower part of the body, you can use either the pure belly breathing or the chest/belly combination. However, if you have major body tensions you want to remove, the following exercise will be helpful.

Sit in the lotus position or lay down on your back, with knees bent and your feet on the floor. Use one of the breathing techniques described above to help release the tension. Quietly get in touch with yourself. Breathe slowly and easily for three to five minutes. When you inhale, visualize your energy moving up, and when you exhale, see the energy moving down towards your feet. While exhaling, you can open your mouth and vocalize a small 'Aahhh' sound.

After several minutes, consciously open up your anus and shift your pelvis slightly backward when you inhale slowly and deeply. When you exhale, move the pelvis slightly forward and send the energy towards your feet.

While inhaling, try to 'breathe into' your area of tension. Become aware of the emotions, images and thoughts which may come to the surface. Continue to exhale towards your feet. If you wish, press and massage the area of tension with your hand as you exhale, continuing to be aware of any emotions which may be released.

If you find that this type of breathing and massage does not remove your tensions, take a hot bath in mineral salts for at least twenty minutes. While you are taking your bath, do the previous exercise again. The combination of breathing, massage and bath (when coupled with a deep awareness of your emotions and feelings) should bring you to a state of total relaxation.

When deep emotions or strong mental images come to the surface, it is best to allow them to be expressed. You may feel like crying without apparent reason, or you may need to punch some pillows in order to move through feelings of anger or aggression. Use a notebook to record your experiences and impressions after working with your breathing and exercise. This will help you get in touch with mental and emotional patterns, and enable you to better integrate your experiences in a clear and grounded way.

During this process you may realize that you need a professional to help you move through this opening process. However, the best helper is your inner truth. Whether you choose to utilize the help of a therapist or not, it is your inner authority which will determine your real direction.

Working with our inner power spots involves a total restructuring of our physical, emotional and mental natures, and lays the foundation for the important work we will experience in our outer power spots in nature. For that reason, we need to be extremely careful and gentle with ourselves. Impatience, impulsiveness, and wilfulness involve 'pushing the river' and are alien to this process of spiritual unfoldment and self-realization. In nature, everything flows at its own rate, and does not need to be hurried or pushed.

It is true that we need to work on ourselves, but this particular path requires self-love, self-nurturing and an extraordinary gentleness. If we can learn to find our resonance with the rhythms of nature, we can walk in harmony with the Earth Mother. And as a result, we will receive Her healing and protection.

Chapter 5

FINDING YOUR OUTER POWER SPOTS

When most people view a waterfall, mountain or tree, they see only the physical manifestation. However, to those who are more sensitive, trees, mountains and lakes contain many subtle dimensions that can be perceived through inner sight. To the extent that we have reached a higher level of consciousness, the greater is our ability to perceive other levels of existence.

Such an idea is nothing new. Trees, lakes, mountains and other aspects of nature have played an important role in the ceremonial and religious life of many ancient cultures throughout the world including the Hebrews (Mount Sinai), the Buddhists (the Bodhi Tree), and the Incas (Macchu Picchu and Lake Titicaca). Among many Indian tribes in North America, the mountaintop would be the preferred place for the sacred *vision quest*, while caves, valleys and waterfalls have always played an important part in major ceremonial and religious rites.

Even on an everyday level, many Westerners have perceived at one time or another, the subtler qualities of nature which go beyond the traditional five senses. As children we often had our 'favourite tree' which offered a sense of strength, stability and protection. Many of us have frequently returned to a certain spot along a stream or river when we need to relax, collect our thoughts, or get into deeper contact with ourselves. Others have experienced the soft yet powerful energy of the ocean, which is both invigorating and calming to the body and the spirit.

By learning to work with power spots, we come into much deeper contact with these subtle forces in nature. Beyond perceiving a mild sensation of peace or protection, we open ourselves consciously to the more potent wisdom and healing power which reside in rocks, mountains and lakes. We also learn how to co-operate with these forces in nature to help us reach deeper levels of self-understanding and inner alignment. As we learn more about *who we really are*, we discover why we are on this planet and where we need to go. This leads us to a clear understanding of our task in life, and how we can make our small yet unique contribution to the evolution of the planet in total harmony and co-operation with all kingdoms of nature.

The first qualification for working with outer power spots is that we must feel truly called to do this work. Rather than making a mental decision because working with nature forms may be interesting or exciting, we need to feel a deep yearning in our hearts to commune with and work with nature. Otherwise, we are merely fooling ourselves, and our efforts would inevitably lead to disappointment.

As with the physical evolution of life on this planet, there is a parallel evolution among the subtler realms of nature. Like human beings, some nature beings are more evolved than others and possess greater intelligence, deeper wisdom, and a more developed sense of compassion and caring. To the degree that we purify our thoughts, understand our emotions and reach a state of natural humility, we are able to attract and work with the more evolved forces in nature. The reason this is important is because unrecognized or unresolved negativities within ourselves can attract corresponding negative forces from the subtle realms of nature.

For this reason, the second qualification is *goodwill*. Our attitude must be one of truly aspiring to resolve those inner issues which block the heart feelings and which prevent us from being in truth in our lives. Although we may not have reached perfection, goodwill, compassion and a sincere desire to serve will all naturally attract the benign energies of nature which protect us and guide us on our journey.

The third necessity is prayer. From a place of true humility, we need to ask for the protection of the Creator, as well as from our inner guides and guardian spirits. We also need to pray to our personal male and female orishas for their guidance in our search, and to ask them to reveal themselves to us.

If these three conditions are met, we will be protected as we proceed on our path, even if we go through periods of difficulty and challenge.

Although the categories are not clear-cut, there are basically three types of outer power spots in nature. *Personal power spots* are places in nature which contain a high concentration of energy which we as individuals resonate with. Candomblé teaches that each person has two personal power spots: one male and one female. These power spots are related to energies that come from the vibration of different elements in nature, such as a waterfall, cliff or mountaintop.

If I find my power spot by a stream, for example, *any stream* has the potential for containing my personal power spot. As we discussed in Chapter 3, the personal power spot is deeply connected with our orisha. The major thrust of this chapter is to help us find our personal power spots as well as our orishas.

Minor power spots are specific natural forms which attract us. While not as powerful as our personal power spots, they contain benign energies which we resonate with. What is a minor power spot for one person can be a personal power spot for another. The distinction lies in the strength of our resonance with the element to which we are attracted.

For example, my two power spots are mountaintops and waterfalls. However, if I am in a field or meadow and have no means of contacting my personal power spots, I may find a place by a tree or an outcrop of rocks with which I resonate. The orishas connected with these minor power spots can bring comfort and help in self-healing and meditation, even though they may not be 'my' male or female orishas.

Planetary power spots are places on earth with extremely powerful concentrations of energy. They can be related to only one orisha, or they can be connected with several. Mount Shasta in California, for example, is one such power spot. It not only receives the vibration of Oshala (the orisha of mountaintops) but also Shangó (who resnoates with thunder, rocks and caves) and Yansan (the orisha of wind and lightning).

A partial listing of planetary power spots includes:

Iguassu Falls (Brazil and Argentina)
Galápagos Islands (Ecuador)
Niagara Falls (USA and Canada)
Ayers Rock (Australia)
Moana Loa Volcano (Hawaii)
Mount Everest (Nepal)
Macchu Picchu (Peru)
Victoria Falls (Zambia)
Stonehenge (England)
Mount Fuji (Japan)

DISCOVERING OUR MALE AND FEMALE ORISHAS

As we mentioned in Chapter 3, the orishas are expressions of the vibration of the energy of different elements in nature. One of the tasks involved in our finding our personal outer power spots is to find both our male and female orishas through the discovery of the earth element (such as a waterfall, cliff or mountaintop) which is connected to each one. When we find our orishas, we also find our corresponding male energy and female energy personal power spots. In order to do this, we have prepared the following ritual which has been utilized extensively in workshops both in Brazil and the United States.

Preparation

1. Choose a place in nature with a maximum variety of the following elements:

mountain	wind
river or stream	trees, woods
waterfall	bare earth
outcrops of rock	ocean
caves	lake, pond, swamp
cliffs	open field on sunny morning

Ideally, you should do this exploration on a warm, sunny day either by yourself or with others. However, the actual discovery of your power spot entails, by necessity, that you are alone.

2. When you awake on the day of your journey, take a shower to cleanse both your physical body and energetic field. For those who may be tense or nervous, a warm bath with mineral or relaxing salts (often available at natural foods stores) is highly recommended before the shower. If a shower is not available, a sponge bath is sufficient.

3. Dress in a light-coloured (preferably white) bathing outfit on top of which you should wear light coloured clothing, which should also be white if possible. *Never* wear black.

4. Take a clay or wooden bowl that has never been used except perhaps for *smudging* purposes. Smudging is the process of cleansing one's energy field with smoke. Long practised by the Roman Catholic Church and the American Indians (among others), smudging involves immersing yourself in the sacred smoke. For our purposes, we suggest burning sage (available at grocery and spice stores) in combination with sweetgrass, pine needles or cedar chips. Place some sage in the bowl and light it, and soon after doing this gently add small amounts of the other ingredient of your choice. When the smoke begins to rise, bring the smoke to your head, face, arms, chest, back, legs and feet with your hands or a feather, as shown in figure 5.1.

5. After you are smudged, light a white candle which has never been used before. While holding your candle, make a prayer to the Creator, your spirit guides and guardian spirits for protection and support. Include a special prayer to your male and female orishas for their guidance and ask that they may reveal themselves to you.

Since this candle should continue to burn after you have left in search of your power spot, be certain that it will not be disturbed or can cause a fire (for this reason many people use candles that are already encased in a glass). In the context of our ritual, this candle will help you on the inner planes while you are praying at your power spot after you have found it.

The Ritual

1. Go to the area in nature you have chosen, and perform all the exercises described in the previous chapter. This will help you open your inner power spots.

2. After you feel that you have made contact with your inner power spots and are in your vertical dimension, close your eyes. If you are alone, begin to spin yourself around until you feel that you have lost your sense of direction. If you are with someone else, close your eyes and ask your companion to lead you to a place you are not familiar with. Ask him/her to turn you around until you lose your sense of direction.

Figure 5.1

When you have lost your sense of direction, continue to spin around (in slow motion) and try to intuit which direction is calling you. When you find this direction, open your eyes just enough so that you see where you are stepping (you should be looking down at your feet rather than straight ahead). Begin calling your name out loud. Some prefer calling out only their first name, while others feel more comfortable calling out both their given and family names. Either way is fine.

Continue to walk in your chosen direction. While you may need to negotiate certain obstacles (like rocks or trees) try to continue moving forward slowly. If you need to move around a rock or a tree, try to reorientate yourself so that you will continue walking in your chosen direction afterwards. Keep calling out your name continuously. Try — as much as possible — to commune with nature with your heart feelings rather than through the rational mind.

The moment will come when you feel you have arrived. Close your eyes. Do not try to analyse or figure out where you are or why. Try to feel the communication between you and that place. Breathe slowly and deeply several times. If you feel a change in your energetic field (or a change in your emotional level or even a change in consciousness) you are almost certain to have found one of your power spots. If you have indeed found your power spot, chances are that you will know it. Then open your eyes and see which element in nature you are resonating with.

You may wish to light a small candle you have carried with you to acknowledge your arrival. You may also want to give a prayer of thanks for the guidance and protection the orisha has given you. Ask your orisha for continued protection and guidance in the work you will do together in full consciousness.

The entire process we have described in this chapter can involve several hours of intense activity. For some people, finding their personal power spot can take much longer and may require several visits. For this reason, it is better that you do not begin working in your power spot immediately on discovering it.

Instead, you should use this opportunity to become familiar with your power spot. This not only involves being physically in contact with it, but becoming aware of your energetic connection to both the power spot and the orisha associated with it. You are, in essence, making a conscious acknowledgement of a relationship which you may have intuitively felt since childhood, but are rediscovering and reclaiming at this time.

Coming into contact with our power spot in nature can be an experience of sheer delight. For many people, it represents the first true sense of fulfilment that they have ever felt. Others may experience a hightened sense of excitement and a state of integration with the Earth. They feel that they have finally 'come home'.

In the following chapter, we will explore how we can actively work in our personal power spots in nature, and how it can be one of the most exciting and rewarding aspects of this path of self-unfoldment.

Chapter 6

WORKING IN YOUR POWER SPOT

Now you know the earth element which your power spot is connected with. Knowing that, you also know your orisha.

As mentioned in the previous chapter, it is not necessary to begin working in your power spot immediately. In fact, it is advisable to devote some time to making deep natural contact with your personal power spot and becoming familiar with the energy of your orisha.

When you are ready to return to your power spot, you may wish to bring an offering to your orisha. Offerings have long played a role in Candomblé teachings (and in other native traditions as well) and are believed to be an important aspect of making contact with and working with one's orisha. There are many different types of offerings one can bring an orisha, but the following gifts, arranged according to each orisha, are especially recommended.

OSHALA

Oshala is the orisha of mountaintops. The suggested offering for Oshala includes white flowers (preferably chrysanthemums) and cooked white corn. You will also need a white piece of cloth (the size of a table mat) that has never been used, two small ceramic or glass candleholders (white or transparent), two white candles, a white porcelain or ceramic bowl (which has never been used before) and, if you wish, a small clear or white vase for the flowers.

The proper method to prepare your offering is as follows: Place the cloth on the ground next to you while you sit in your power spot. Fill the bowl with the cooked corn to be set in the centre of the cloth. Place the flowers in the vase and set it by the bowl, or arrange the flowers around the bowl of corn either directly on the cloth, or as shown in figure 6.1 Set the candlesticks on either side of the bowl.

Figure 6.1

SHANGÓ

Shangó is the orisha of rocks, cliffs, caves and thunder. He is said to like red flowers, white and red (or white and red striped) candles, and reddish fruits like apples, plums and pomegranates. Candomblé priests suggest placing the fruits in a new while clay or porcelain bowl, although it is permissible to lay them on a new white tablecloth. The flowers can be arranged around the bowl of fruit directly on the cloth, and the candles can be affixed directly to a rock or to the ground. While the candles and flowers are considered to be important offering, the fruits need not be offered every time you visit a power spot of Shangó.

OMOLU

Candomblé teaches that Omolu is connected with bare earth under direct sunlight, as well as open fields with sparce vegetation. As mentioned earlier, one should work with Omolu *only* during the morning while the sun is rising and *never* after the noon hour.

As with the offerings described before, you will need a 'virgin' white bowl made of clay or porcelain, a new white cloth, white or clear candleholders, and, optionally, a vase for the flowers. Cooked popcorn (prepared without salt, butter or other additives) should be placed in the bowl, and white flowers should be placed either in the vase or arranged around the bowl and laid directly on the cloth. It is recommended that when you make an offering to Omolu, the two candles should be white and maroon in colour.

OSHUNMARÉ

Oshunmaré is the orisha connected with rainbows, although water is the main element to use when you wish to communicate with Him. When making an offering to Oshunmare, it is recommended that you choose a stream, pond, or other inland body of water. Your flowers should represent as many of the colours of the rainbow as possible, and can be arranged on a 'virgin' white cloth placed next to the water. White or multi-coloured candles are also suggested when you make an offering to this orisha.

OSHOSSI

Oshossi is the orisha connected with wooded areas, forests and orchards. According to the teachings of Candomblé, Oshossi responds best to offerings of sliced coconut and green and red fruits like apples, pears, avocados and papayas. Cooked red corn (if available) is also suggested, in addition to white and light blue flowers and candles.

Place your offering of fruits in a new white bowl, which is to be laid on a white or light blue cloth selected especially for this purpose. Place one white and one blue candle (or two white and blue striped candles) in white or transparent candleholders, and arrange them around the offering of fruit. Like the offering to Oshala, the flowers should be placed in a white or transparent vase, or may simply be arranged on the cloth around the bowl of fruit.

OGOUN

Ogoun is the orisha of iron, and can be found in deep woods and especially near outcroppings and veins of iron. In addition to a white and dark blue table mat, the candleholders and an unused white or unglazed clay bowl, the primary offering to Ogoun consists of toasted dry black beans. A white and blue candle (or two striped white and dark blue candles) are also recommended. Prepare your offering as described earlier.

YEMANJÁ

Yemanjá rules the oceans, and the offerings made to Her are considered the most exotic and beautiful among those given to orishas. They include white flowers (especially roses), white candles, and women's perfume. Offerings can be made in several ways.

One method calls for going to the beach and digging a hole in the sand in which you will place offerings of candles and flowers. The hole should be deep enough to protect the lighted candles from the wind. There is no limit to the number of candles you can use — this should depend on your intuition. Many pilgrims prefer to arrange the candles around the flowers. Open the bottle of perfume and place it near the centre of the offering.

You can also make your offering by simply walking into the ocean carrying a bouquet of white flowers. Begin making your prayer or request to Yemanja as soon as you enter the water, and count the number of waves that wash by. After you meet the seventh wave, cast your flowers (either all together or one by one) into the surf to be received by Yemanja.

OSHOUN

Oshoun is the orisha of flowing fresh waters, and is found at waterfalls, rivers and streams. Her favourite offerings include yellow flowers (especially yellow roses) and white and yellow candles.

One form of offering consists of placing the flowers on a 'virgin' white or yellow table-mat-sized cloth as close to the water as possible. If you are using the cloth (which is optional) you should place the candles in the type of candleholders described earlier. However, the flowers and candles can also be placed directly on the ground.

The other recommended form of making an offering to Oshoun involves standing by the stream or waterfall, making your prayers, and casting the flowers into the water.

NANAN

Unlike Oshoun, Nanan is the orisha of still fresh waters and is connected to ponds and marshy areas. Cooked popcorn (prepared without additives) is considered the primary offering to Nanan, along with flowers that are white or aquamarine blue in colour. The candles may either be white, aquamarine blue, or a combination of both. Candleholders and a white or deep blue cloth are optional, although a white bowl (which has never been used) is needed for the popped corn. The offerings are to be placed on the shore as close to the water as possible, as seen in figure 6.2.

Figure 6.2

YANSAN

Yansan is connected with wind and lightning, and is believed to be present in naturally windy places. Unlike the other orishas, who are found primarily in areas uninhabited by human beings, Yansan can be found wherever there is wind, including the roofs of buildings and the decks of ships.

White and red flowers are said to be favoured by this orisha, as are red and white candles. Since you will be making your offering in a windy place, it is a good idea to surround your candle by glass or find a votive-type candle available in church supply stores and some supermarkets and *botánicas*. The flowers can be simply laid by the candles to be carried off by Yansan.

CLOTHING

When you journey to your power spot to visit your orisha, the colour of your clothing is very important. White or light-coloured clothing is preferred, although you can also add the particular colour of your orisha (in the form of a necklace, scarf or ribbon) to a white outfit. *Never wear black or solely dark colours when you visit your outer power spot.*

The following colours are suggested for working with the orishas, and should be worn if possible, *along with white.*

Male	Female
Oshala — white only	Yemanjá — white only
Shangó — white or burgundy	Oshoun — yellow
Omolu — white or dark red/brown	Nanan — aquamarine blue
Oshunmaré — rainbow colours	Yansan — red
Oshossi — light blue	
Ogoun — dark blue	

In addition to your offering and clothing, it is always a practical idea to bring along some drinking water, matches and other incidentals which you may require when taking a journey to nature.

You may also wish to carry a *rock crystal* with you when you visit your power spot to work with your orisha. Among the American Indians, crystals are believed to impart certain beneficial energies to those who carry them or wear them as jewellery. There are many kinds of crystals available, but we recommend one of the following: clear quartz (to connect with higher and/or deeper levels of consciousness), amethyst (to transform and transmute energy), rose quartz (to calm the emotions and to open up and nurture love energies) and smokey quartz (for grounding and mental clarity).*

---

*You can learn more about crystals and their powers from *Cosmic Crystals* by Ra Bonewitz (Wellingborough: Turnstone Press Ltd, 1983).

IN YOUR POWER SPOT

When you return to your power spot, the first task is to ground yourself. After placing your offerings aside, you can either stand up or sit down, getting in touch with the earth and feeling your vertical dimension. You are aligned, aware and inwardly calm.

You may also wish to perform some exercises to increase contact with both the ground and your inner power spots. Deep breathing, meditation and prayer are all recommended as you move towards your inner core or centre. It is important to remember that contact with orishas and other nature beings is not made through the rational mind, but through the intuition. Your main challenge is to follow it and move in whatever direction your intuition leads.

Although many things can happen when we work with our orisha, this work usually takes one of two primary directions. The first direction involves self-exploration. The goal is to reach deep levels of consciousness within. You may begin this process by making contact with your inner power spots, or you can work with meditation, deep breathing or chanting. Then, follow your intuition regarding what to do next in the areas of body movement, behaviour, emotions or thought. If your power spot is by a lake, for example, you may choose to spend several hours immersed in the water singing, swimming or otherwise moving about. On the other hand, you may decide to remain on the shore and practise deep meditation sitting in the lotus position.

When you feel that you are actually in touch with your orisha, you may also want to ask questions concerning your personality, major decisions you need to make, or the direction you are to take in your life. You can also ask your orisha to help you work through psychological or psychic blocks, areas of destructive behaviour, and other life patterns which limit you and prevent you from reaching your full potential.

The other direction of work with our orisha involves respectfully asking Him/Her to help us resolve a specific difficulty we may have. We often have moments of crisis which manifest as a serious problem with work, a difficult relationship, financial reversals, spiritual doubts, or a disease or other physical problem. In many ways, a crisis can provide a valuable learning experience and enables us to focus on certain areas of disharmony in our lives which require our attention. For this reason, it is important to explore the *symbolic meaning* that a particular crisis may have to offer us, and why it is taking place at this particular moment in our lives.

For many people, the primary goal in dealing with a crisis is its immediate resolution, without wanting to understand the deeper meaning it may have for us. When a crisis is resolved in this way, if often reappears at a later time. When working with an orisha, some people prefer to ask for help in ending the outer manifestation of a crisis for the time being without seeking to work with it on a deeper level.

However, others have learned that it is far more important to ask the orisha to help us understand the deeper meaning of a crisis, and to enable us to work through it so that a deep genuine healing can take place through the transformation of consciousness. As a result, a heavy burden becomes much easier to deal with and a major problem can be resolved once and for all.

Whichever of the two paths you choose, you must be in alignment with your vertical dimension. After you feel that you are grounded, aligned and integrated in your power spot and are resonating with your orisha, you can reverently make your offering by carefully laying out your foods, flowers and candles in the manner described earlier. If candles are a part of your offering, you may light them at this time. The offering should remain in your power spot when you leave, but you may wish to extinguish your candles to avoid a possible fire.

Make your prayer. Pray first to your orisha, and then make a prayer to Oshala (the 'father' of the orishas), a prayer for all orishas, a prayer to all forms in the spirit world and to the energies and powers of the earth. Make a prayer to your personal spirit guides followed by a prayer to God or the Great Spirit who created all things.

A WORD OF CAUTION

As we mentioned in Chapter 3, the subtle realms of existence are populated with a wide variety of beings at different stages of evolution. When we are working in these realms, certain entities may sometimes be attracted to us. They come through the gate of the resonance of energies within us, so we only attract energies with which we resonate. By following the guidelines mentioned in this chapter, chances are slim that you will attract any negative or otherwise disharmonious beings when you are in your power spot.

However, if you do attract some spirit being, ask yourself 'What is in me that attracts this force?' Although some of the forces in the subtle realms are quite benign, others are not, even though they may appear to be beautiful, enlightened or otherwise appealing. Whenever you meet a spirit being in the subtle realms, you need to follow your intuition regarding its intent. If you have any doubts at all, speak from your innermost being 'If you come in the name of God, you are welcome. If not, please go away.' This should be followed with a prayer to God for protection and clarity.

If you had any doubts, they should be resolved at this point. However in very rare cases, negative spirits may still remain, but after making your prayer to God, you will know that they are negative. Continue making your prayer to God and send them away. At the same time, however, take responsibility for the aspect in you which is attracting this entity. Be aware of the energy within you which is attracting a similar energy from outside. Continue to pray and ask it to leave.

We have not presented this material to scare you, nor to prevent you from working with your orishas. However, by choosing to work in the subtle realms, you are entering a world which you may not be at all familiar with — a world with its own inhabitants, forces and terrain.

Like a traveller's guidebook which tells you about customs regulations, tipping, ground transportation and hotel accommodation when you first enter a foreign country, this chapter is intended to guide you as you first enter into the subtle realms of existence. However, the journey you will take after this point will unfold naturally through your own inner guidance. You will follow your own itinerary, and will create your own unique adventure.

Chapter 7

SELF-TRANSFORMATION AND PLANETARY HEALING

In the preceding chapters we have presented a path of spiritual growth that integrates working with oneself (through our inner power spots) with the wisdom of the orishas, found in our outer power spots in nature. At the same time, we have offered the essential tools needed to travel on this path and to be open to the insights and personal healing it can provide. The goal has been to help us find our task in life and to understand our own unique place in the world as a child of the Earth Mother.

Discovering our identity as a child of the Earth Mother can open up a completely new world for those of us who choose to explore it. In addition to personal unfoldment and inner healing, communication with the forces of nature can eventually empower us to build a new society that will resonate both with natural and universal law. By returning to our roots and learning how to live in harmony with the Earth, we can end our long period of alienation from the land and begin to aid in the healing of this planet.

The danger of extinction of both the Earth Mother and Her children is real. Nuclear winters, 'Star Wars' military technology, five thousand people dying from starvation daily in Northern Africa, or an entire forest decimated by acid rain — all speak of humanity's alienation from the Earth Mother, our very source of sustenance, protection and support.

When we begin to work with power spots and nature forces, we soon begin to realize that humanity's destruction of nature is an expression of our ignorance of our own inner nature. It reveals a lack of awareness, a fear to stand by the truth, and the desire to avoid taking responsibility for our lives. It is also an expression of a lack of personal grounding and the stubborn maintenance of our masks.

For the most part, ungrounded people are competitive, jealous, greedy and insecure, and build a society that is equally so. Living in this way, we also choose and empower others to take on the role of leaders in areas such as politics, business and religion. In many cases, these authority figures are more ungrounded than most people, and make important decisions that are often not in truth and show no regard for the long-term effects that their decisions can have on the Earth Mother. Like most members of society, these people function primarily from a mask level, and are often completely out of touch with their inner reality.

Genuine or true power does not reside in masks. Real power has nothing to do with covering insecurity with rationality and macho displays of force. Nor does it involve the manipulation of people's emotions calling for nationalism, militarism, racism or religious separatism. True power is the force that a person channels from the universe through the vertical dimension, grounded in love and compassion.

The person who wields true power is not only grounded, but can experience both the energy of the universe and the pulsations of the earth. In reality, such an individual is a bridge between the forces of heaven and earth, and blends spiritual vision with practicality and realism. While this person can exercise great power, it is only used for purposes that encourage co-operation, truth and harmony. That person is a living channel for what Albert Schweitzer called 'the will to good'.

However, achieving this state of being is the result of many years of deep personal work. It involves progressively discovering who we really are. For this to occur, we need to be aware of the compulsive and repetitive patterns in our lives. We need to transform the masks we have used to hide our real selves from ourselves and others. Such a process leads us to gradually assume full resonsibility for our lives rather than blaming others or God, and expecting them to resolve our problems.

As we reach deeper and deeper layers of consciousness, we move closer to discovering the core of our real being, which is the centre of our wisdom, creativity and inner strength. As a result, we increase the possibility of making contact with the essence of true human nature: the triad of Will, Knowledge and Love.

As we mentioned before, this work is the result of the marriage of both the horizontal and vertical dimensions within us. It involves not only working in our power spots (which can be highly effective in its own right) but bringing the knowledge and wisdom which has come to us through our experience in these energy centres into daily life.

The true power of the grounded and integrated individual is potentially far stronger than that of a demagogue. By constantly utilizing true power in our personal lives, we can have an important impact on the world around us. Being grounded in nature and working with natural forces gives us both a more physical energy and mental focus, and we are able to function with greater freedom and clarity. We learn how to face doubt, fears and challenges squarely and with courage. We function from the centre of our being.

As a result, we not only begin to transform our relationships, but we begin to discover the deeper, more spiritual aspects of work, study and community service. We also become deeply aware of our intimate connection with the earth and the responsibility this knowledge entails.

When many people begin to reclaim their true power and apply it in daily life, the impact on the planetary level can be great. Old expressions of our collective masks — including economic greed, political distortions, militarism and environmental insensitivity — will gradually and naturally be transformed into new ways of being that are based on truth, non-violence and respect for the Earth Mother. On a societal level, all areas of life — including education, economics, agriculture, politics and religion — will be affected by this powerful transformation of collective consciousness and the right application of power.

This will gradually lead to a true healing of the planet as we commit ourselves to our natural role as responsible and caring children of the Earth Mother.

BIBLIOGRAPHY

Albright, Peter and Albert, Betsy Parker, *Body, Mind and Spirit* (Brattleboro, Vt., Stephen Greene Press, 1980).

Baker, Ellsworth, *Man in the Trap* (New York: Macmillan Co., 1977).

Bastide, Roger, *The African Religions of Brazil* (Baltimore: John Hopkins University Press, 1978).

Bendit, L. J. and Phoebe B., *The Etheric Body of Man* (Wheaton, Ill., Quest Books, 1977).

Besant, Annie, *O Homen e os seus corpos (Man and His Bodies)* (São Paulo: Editora Pensamento, 1982).

Booth, Newell S. Jr. (ed.), *African Religions: A Symposium* (New York: NOK Publishers, 1977).

Gunther, Bernard, *Energy, Ecstacy and Your Seven Vital Chakras* (Los Angeles: Guild of Tutors Press, 1978).

Hodson, Geoffrey, *Kingdom of the Gods* (Adyar, Madras: Theosophical Publishing House, 1952).

—— *The Brotherhood of Angels and of Men* (London: Theosophical Publishing House, 1955).

—— *Lecture Notes, Vol. I* (Adyar, Madras: Theosophical Publishing House, 1955).

Keleman, Stanley, *Somatic Reality* (Berkeley: Center Press, 1979).

Leadbeater, C. W., *The Chakras* (Adyar, Madras: Theosophical Publishing House, 1969).

—— *Man Visible and Invisible* (Adyar, Madras: Theosophical Publishing House, 1969).

Lowen, M.D., Alexander, *Physical Dynamics of Character Structure* (New York: Grune & Stratton, 1958).

—— *Bioenergetics* (New York: Coward, McCann, 1975).

—— *The Way to Vibrant Health* (New York: Harper & Row, 1977).

Motoyama, Hiroshi, *Theories of the Chakras: Bridge to Higher Consciousness* (Wheaton, Ill.: Quest Books, 1981).

Ogum, Jair de; *Fé* (Rio de Janeiro: Agents Editores, 1984).

Powell, A. E., *The Etheric Body* (London: Theosophical Publishing House, 1969).
—— *The Mental Body* (London: Theosophical Publishing House, 1967).
Reich, Wilhelm; *Character Analysis* (New York: Farrar, Strauss & Giroux, 1972).
Southern Centre of Theosophy, *Devas and Men* (Adyar, Madras: The Theosophical Publishing House, 1977).
Sun Bear and Wabun, *The Medicine Wheel* (Englewood Cliffs, N.J.: Prentice Hall, 1980).
Tamsley, David V., *Subtle Body* (London: Thames & Hudson, 1972).
Tôrres de Freitas, B. and Cardoso de Freitas, V., *Os Orixás e o Candomblé* (Rio de Janeiro: Editora Eco, 1967).
Verger, Pierre; *Dieux d'Afrique* (Paris: Paul Hartmann Editeur, 1954).

INDEX

Of further interest . . .

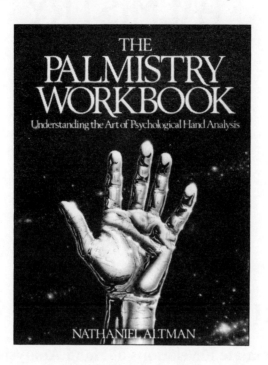

THE PALMISTRY WORKBOOK

Do you know your TRUE psychological nature? Do you have a tendency towards mental illness? Is your health good and will it remain good? Are you developed to your full potential emotionally, sexually and spiritually? Your hands are more expressive, more specific and can reflect the essence of your life with greater depth and accuracy than any other part of your body. **Nathaniel Altman** shows how you can analyse your hand to discover the truth about your personal relationships, sexuality, state of health and ideal career. This is an indispendable guide to psychological hand analysis and is the only book you will ever need on this fascinating subject.

SEXUAL PALMISTRY

The Intimate Revelations of Hand Analysis

What does the colour of your nails reveal about your sex drive? How can you distinguish an honest suitor from a dishonest one? Will he/she be faithful? Is this THE relationship? Whenever anyone visits a palmist the first questions they are likely to ask are about personal relationships — yet until now there has been no book which *solely* explores the extensive ramifications of a sexually orientated reading. **Nathaniel Altman** *here corrects that situation.* In this easy-to-read but remarkably detailed volume, he exposes — for anyone who can read the signs — the most intimate secrets of our psyche.

★ Always choose the right man/woman.
★ Know if the relationship will be satisfactory — or not!
★ Understand the hidden mysteries of your partner's mind . . . with this, the first book *ever* to integrate scientific hand analysis with contemporary sexual psychology.

HOW TO READ HANDS

A Step-by-Step Guide to Modern Hand Analysis

Lori Reid takes a refreshing and stimulating look at the ancient science of palmistry — and a science it really is! For the majority of the population palmistry has been a parlour game — a bit of fun — but Lori Reid shows that there really IS more to it than that. We all know that the mind *can* affect the body — in psychosomatic illness for example — or in the case of a grumpy person who produces a grumpy face — the author argues that if we accept these things as facts, then we should also accept the probability that our hopes and aspirations are reflected in the features of the body — the hands for instance. She introduces the reader, in a chatty yet straightforward style, firstly to the basics of hand analysis and then, in a more thorough way, to the whole absorbing subject of plamistry *including* a section on health in which she shows how the condition of the hands, temperature, nails, skin etc. can give important prior warning of possibly adverse health conditions.

THE FEMALE HAND

"Our lives are marked out in our hands, rather like a road map, and . . . with a little knowledge of the principles of hand analysis we are better able to choose the direction we wish to steer." **Lori Reid's** book is as unique as the female hand itself, being aimed solely at women (women of all ages from all walks of life). Palmistry skills gained from this book will be a blessing to all women — for the young girl in decoding the palms of interviewers, fellow workers and budding boyfriends; for the mother, to tell the true nature and potential of her children and for when the same children leave home, hand analysis can guide towards picking up the threads of abilities neglected, to care for those children. *Includes an abundance of actual examples of hand analysis techniques in conjunction with female case histories.*